GDPR – How to Achieve and Maintain Compliance

Following the implementation of the new General Data Protect Regulation on 25 May 2018, organizations should now be fully compliant with their national interpretation of this far-reaching data protection standard. The reality is that most are not; whether through their inappropriate use of online cookies or ineffective physical data security, businesses continue to struggle with the increasing pressure from regulators to apply the Regulation. Non-compliance is widely due to misinterpretation, lack of real-world thinking, and challenges in balancing costs against business practicalities.

This book provides insight into how to achieve effective compliance in a realistic, no-nonsense and efficient way. The authors have over 100 years' collective international experience in security, compliance and business disciplines and know what it takes to keep companies secure and in-line with regulators' demands. Whether your organization needs to swiftly adopt GDPR standards or apply them in "Business as Usual" this book provides a wide range of recommendations and explicit examples.

With the likelihood of high-profile penalties causing major reputational damage, this book explains how to reduce risk, run a remedial project, and take immediate steps towards mitigating gaps. Written in plain English, it provides an invaluable international reference for effective GDPR adoption.

Andrew Denley is a GDPR Compliance Consultant with 35 years' experience in the research, intelligence, government and commerce sectors in both technical and consultancy capacities. In recent years he has championed and implemented information security risk analysis and framework compliance for a number of commercial companies with considerable success. An ISO27001 Lead Auditor, he has been listed on the International Register for Certified Auditors.

Mark Foulsham is Chief Digital Officer at Scope, CEO of Surrey Innovations, and Director of CIO Connect, UK. He has experience spanning over 30 years in leading both business and technology disciplines within organizations and has supported businesses from the Financial Services, wider commercial sector, universities and social enterprises in achieving their GDPR compliance programmes.

Brian Hitchen is a GDPR Compliance Consultant and author with 30 years' experience working as an IT Security Manager for a number of financial services organizations. With an interest in cyber crime and the impact on small to medium businesses, Brian now writes to help companies better understand IT security, risks and issues, contingency planning and data analysis and plan what they need to do to counter the latest threats and deal with legislation.

GDPR – How to Achieve and Maintain Compliance

Andrew Denley, Mark Foulsham and Brian Hitchen

TRAINING
Outline
- what?   - Penalties
- Why?
- when?
- Rights of data subject
- Data Processer v. Controller
- General Process, & how the tool helps.

Routledge
Taylor & Francis Group

LONDON AND NEW YORK

First published 2019
by Routledge
2 Park Square, Milton Park, Abingdon, Oxon OX14 4RN

and by Routledge
52 Vanderbilt Avenue, New York, NY 10017

Routledge is an imprint of the Taylor & Francis Group, an informa business

British Library Cataloguing-in-Publication Data
A catalogue record for this book is available from the British Library

Library of Congress Cataloging-in-Publication Data
A catalog record has been requested for this book

Visit the eResources: www.Routledge.com/9781138326170

ISBN: 978-1-138-32617-0 (hbk)
ISBN: 978-0-429-44997-0 (ebk)

Typeset in Bembo
by Integra Software Services Pvt. Ltd.

Contents

The Authors

Andrew Denley MBCS With 35 years' experience in sectors covering research, intelligence, government and commerce Andrew has worked in technology all his career, seamlessly moving into IT from Data Communications with the advent of work-place computers and then into Information Security as the use of the Internet expanded. Passionate about information risk and security, he has continuously championed these "necessary evils" as business enablers believing that they sit firmly within the business, rather than IT, function.

Mark Foulsham MBCS Mark has experience spanning over 30 years leading both business and technology disciplines within broad types of organizations. During this time, he has spent his career at the "sharp end" of what it means to provide safe, reliable systems to high-transaction businesses. These include start-ups, recently merged and divested entities, and newly listed companies.

In addition, he has worked with small and medium enterprises (SMEs) to ensure that confidentiality and security provisions are effective at the right level of investment and are not a throttle to an organization's productivity.

Mark has a strong presence in his industry peer group and in 2014 was a finalist in the INSEAD European CIO of the Year Award. From 2004– 2016 Mark was CIO for esure Insurance Group (including the comparison site GoCompare) – one of the fastest growing internet insurers of recent times. In his 12-year tenure there were no serious data breaches or cyber-attacks – he puts this down to putting security at the centre of every aspect of business thinking. During this time Mark was also a non-executive director for Europe's largest Exchange cloud hosting business, Cobweb, and chaired the Advisory Board of CIO Connect.

More recently as part of a portfolio of engagements, Mark has supported businesses from the financial services, wider commercial sector, universities, and social enterprises in achieving their GDPR compliance programmes. Mark also provides coaching to CIOs and CTOs.

Brian Hitchen MBCS Brian worked in IT from 1970 until 2014. He spent the last 30 years working as IT Security Manager for a number of financial services organizations. In 1995 he trained and installed a cyber forensics facility as part of his security role; this was one of the first to be used in the commercial sector in the UK. Since then he has investigated several high-value financial crimes.

In 2014 he retired from full-time work and has since been researching cyber crime and the impact that it has on small to medium businesses. He has co-written *Disaster Avoidance* and *Hacked!*, both available from Amazon. He has written a series of reports for the House of Lords while the Investigatory Powers Bill was being reviewed.

He is a best-selling author, volunteers as a STEM Ambassador, and with his local branch of the National Coast Watch and helps fundraise for his local Lifeboat.

Brian is a member of the British Computer Society and on the committee of the Sussex Branch.

Acknowledgements

The GDPR consists of 99 Articles and 173 Recitals. The Recitals clarify or expand the wording of the Articles so if you want a full understanding of the GDPR you need to read the Articles alongside the Recitals.

In the course of conducting research for this book we discovered a very helpful list of the Articles with the Recitals that relate to them. We found these so helpful, along with their unofficial descriptions, that we asked for permission to reproduce them in this book. We are grateful to **Intersoft Consulting** for allowing us to use their material and happily acknowledge them as the authors of this work. Please see www.intersoft-consulting.de or their website and www.gdpr-info.eu for the layout of the Articles and Recitals that appear in Section 14 (The Regulation) in this book.

Introduction

This book is aimed at both EU and non-EU organizations and explains how to comply with the General Data Protection Regulation (GDPR) without necessarily having to change the way that your whole organization operates.

When considering the risk of litigation those organizations that are based in the US and are in-scope for GDPR should be particularly wary. Given the high degree of non-compliance and readiness (according to an ISACA survey in May 2018, only 29% of participants were aware of the GDPR) as well as the prevalence of a litigious culture, there is potentially a perfect storm in the USA which could lead to many organizations being fined directly by regulators or taken to court by individuals and non-business groups. As US businesses become more conversant and compliant with the Regulation, this risk will clearly decline but 2018–2019 Is likely to be a period in which high-profile test cases will influence progress in this regard. Solutions to seek out non-compliance using tools such as AI technology and (Robotic Networks) to trawl companies' public content will also act as a catalyst to legal action in the USA and globally.

Structure of this book

The book is in 14 parts which we have called "Sections" and Section 14 contains the GDPR text. This is divided into "Chapters" so to avoid having two entries called Chapter 1, for example, we have used Sections to divide our text. Within Section 14 the GDPR has 99 Acts and 173 Recitals. The European Commission decided to include Recitals in the legislation to provide examples and clarity for the Articles. We have therefore listed the recital number for each of the Articles so that you can look these up if you need them but have not included the wording as we felt that this would make the book too long.

We refer to the UK Data Protection Acts 1998 and 2018 a great deal in this book. This is because the UK was an early adopter of privacy legislation and the

Information Commissioner's Office (the ICO – the UK Regulator) has provided significant advice to businesses. The Data Protection Act (DPA) 2018 has the GDPR as the starting point and clarifies and expands on some of the issues. The ICO regularly publishes advice and guidance on the nature and application of both the UK 2018 Data Protection Act as well as the GDPR. We therefore refer to these documents where we feel they are the best source of information.

The book can be read in part or in whole – it is intended to be a companion reference to your alignment with the GDPR.

Italic text

Where we quote the Regulation or a Government Body within the test we will place the quoted material in italics to indicate that we are quoting an official source.

The journey of GDPR to statute

The GDPR was passed in the 28 member-countries of the EU on 14 April 2016 and came into force 20 days later. There was then a two-year transition period to give organizations time to comply with the requirements. The Regulation came into force on 25 May 2018 at which time any organization that processes or stores personal data, which is often referred to as personally identifiable information (PII), belonging to any living citizen of, or any living individual residing in the EU must comply with the Regulation. As for the term personal data, as used in the EU and which may be seen to have a slightly different meaning to PII, we will use "personal data" throughout this book as this is the term used in the GDPR and in the UK Data Protection Legislation. As the UK was a member of the EU at the time of the Regulation becoming law it automatically became UK law and had the same transition time as the rest of the EU. Because the UK later voted to leave the EU the Great Repeal Bill then removed the EU laws from the UK statute book. However, on 13 September 2017 the UK published the UK Data Protection Bill (2017) which brought the GDPR into UK law. The Data Protection Act (2018) was passed into UK law on 23 May 2018 and the effect of this was to make the GDPR apply to UK organizations even after Brexit, and while there are some small changes to the wording of the Articles the main thrust of the GDPR remains the same and all UK companies that process personal data will have to comply with the requirements of the GDPR.

Even though there was a two-year transition period many companies failed to act in a timely manner or, for the smaller organizations, were unaware of the new legislation. To make matters worse many organizations that were aware of the Regulations saw the GDPR as an "IT issue" which was missing the point. While IT will probably have a large input into the project you should not rely on your IT team to run it. The GDPR has organization-wide implications and needs to be a project that engages with all departments. In practice this means that IT will not be able to decide, for example, which records are no longer needed, nor the retention policy for Marketing, HR, Accounts etc. These decisions can only be made by the departments that own the data.

Penalties

The GDPR places far greater requirements on companies to manage and protect their data and significantly expands the scope of protection which can trigger substantial punitive measures for non-compliance. Under the 1998 Data Protection Act (DPA) the maximum fine for a breach was £500,000 and most European countries could levy fines that were comparable. Under the GDPR the maximum fine for a serious breach is 20 million euros (or the sterling equivalent based on the exchange rate on the day of the fine) or 4% of the previous year's global turnover, whichever is higher, and while this would only be levied for the most serious of breaches there is also provision for any data subject who has suffered "material or non-material damage as a result of an infringement of this Regulation" to have "the right to receive compensation from the controller or processor for the damage suffered" (Article 82(1)).

It should be noted that there is a lesser fine – up to 10 million euros or 2% of annual turnover – if there is an infringement of Article 8 (child's consent) or Article 11 (processing that does not require identification). Article 83 provides the full definition for imposing fines.

Practical application

Knowing how to adhere to the new regulation in a practical and affordable manner will be key to meeting GDPR requirements without undue burden.

To assist in achieving pragmatic compliance, this book will:

- provide clarity on what the Regulation means, in plain English and where appropriate in layman's terms;
- give practical steps within the key Articles to ensure readiness;
- highlight the possible pitfalls to avoid along your journey;
- describe how you should communicate, plan and execute your changes in a controlled manner;
- explain what you should expect to achieve in order to comply with the regulation.

GDPR history

As corporations have grown ever larger and the IT systems that they use have included more data, various countries have legislated to protect the privacy of their citizens. In the UK the first Data Protection Act was passed in 1984 and introduced a series of definitions to protect the privacy of a "Data Subject". The definition of a data subject was and is "a living individual who can be identified". The Act was passed at a time when the public were becoming concerned about the amount of data that computer bureaus were collecting. At that time data was collected and processed on large mainframe computers that were housed in vast computer rooms that had very few connections to other computers. The Internet was not available to the public (that would not happen until 1991) and although personal computers were available, these were not connected to the rest of the world. There was no social media and no known computer virus had been written (that would not happen until 1990 when the IBM world-wide mainframe network was brought to a halt by the "Christmas Tree" Virus).

The aim of the Act was to ensure that any data collected was accurate and kept up to date, with the main focus on ensuring that data was complete and not excessive. The original 1984 Act mentioned "Security" on six occasions but there was no mention of "sensitive personal data". The 1998 Act was introduced into a world that had seen the start of the Internet, the first personal computers (Apple and IBM) were being mass-produced and companies were starting to build an Internet presence. Google started in 1996 and Amazon in 1998, so the new Data Protection Act was coming into a rapidly changing cyber world (though the word cyber wasn't used in the context of a computer).

The 1998 Act introduced the Data Protection Principles. These stated that personal data shall:

1. be processed fairly
2. be obtained only for one or more specific lawful purposes
3. be adequate, relevant and not excessive
4. be accurate and, where necessary, kept up to date
5. not be kept for longer than is necessary
6. be processed in accordance with the Act
7. be kept secure
8. not be transferred outside of the EU unless that country has similar protection in place.

While there were new safeguards for data subjects there were a number of gaps in the legislation that companies could exploit. The need for people to consent to data transfers could be hidden in Terms and Conditions with the onus being on the customer to read a lengthy document and they often had to contact the company if they wanted to withdraw their consent. If their data had already been passed on to another organization, the original company had no responsibility to trace the data and delete it. Companies that did give their customers a choice would often present the consent box already ticked, so the customer had to un-tick it if they didn't want their data shared or sent out of the EU.

The UK Data Protection Act 1998 was derived from the EU Data Protection Directive 1995 and (for all its faults), the Act was a leap forward for consumers. Yet while there were abuses there were also many successful prosecutions of companies that failed to comply with the Act. As the EU grew, each member country had their own version of the European Data Protection Directive, and it became clear that some of the new giant corporations that were based in the United States of America were starting to use their financial muscle to avoid costly compliance issues. There were many lengthy court cases and it was clear that the focus of the rights of the individual that was behind much of European legislation was at odds with the American principle that the individual had a duty to take care of themselves and their family. The "Nanny State", as the giant Internet corporations viewed the law, was not something that the average American company bought into. They preferred to offer their services on the basis that the customer was free to choose them or a competitor. The United States government was unwilling to be prescriptive where the corporations were concerned. Eventually, the European view that the consumer needed to have better protection started to swing the argument and the EU decided to create a pan-European Regulation that would protect their citizens.

The following three subsections are key to understanding the way that the book is designed and will help you to get the most out of what we say.

Key roles defined

- Data subject: A living natural person
- Data controller: Specifies how personal data is to be used
- Data processor: Uses the data under the guidance of the Data Controller
- DPO: Data Protection Officer – the person who advises an organization how to comply with the regulation
- EDPB: European Data Protection Board – the coordinating body that provided consistency between SAs
- ICO: Information Commissioner's Office (The SA in the UK)
- SA: Supervisory Authority – a national body (the Information Commissioner in the UK) who enforces the regulation
- Third country: A country outside of the EU
- Third party: an individual linked to a data subject or any company or organization to which data is sent.

GDPR principles

There are seven principles that are the basis of the GDPR, these are:

1. legality, transparency and fairness
2. purpose limitation

3. minimization
4. accuracy
5. storage limitation
6. integrity and confidentiality
7. accountability.

If your organization stores and processes personal data in accordance with these principles, you will be well on the way to complying with the GDPR. These principles are expanded in Section 5 – Your GDPR project.

Your GDPR project

Here are some high-level points that we will go into more detail in the next section.

1. Does the GDPR affect your business?
2. This is a business project, NOT just for IT
3. You will need commitment from the board of directors
4. You should have an Executive Champion
5. You must decide your data types and who owns them
6. The Data Protection Impact Assessment or DPIA
7. Create an action plan
8. The role of IT within the GDPR
9. Reviewing what data your suppliers hold
10. Reviewing your current privacy practices and creating a governance structure
11. Reviewing your right to process
12. What to do if you have an incident.

Section
1

Does the GDPR apply to you?

As the GDPR came into European law, not unsurprisingly, there has been some confusion about to whom the law actually applies and this consternation has been fuelled by mis-reporting in the national press and on social media groups.

First and foremost, the GDPR applies to any business that collects, retains or processes personal data belonging to a living individual residing in Europe. If you are an individual who has personal data of someone you know (with their permission) on a personal computing device, then the GDPR does not apply to you.

- If you run a club or private society that retains personal data of other members (again with their permission), then the GDPR does not apply to you.
- If you are self-employed as a consultant to a business, then the GDPR does not apply to you.
- If you are self-employed running your own business and you collect, process and/or retain personal data, then the GDPR does apply to you.
- If you collect, process and/or retain personal data belonging to a natural living person and they reside outside of the EU, then the GDPR does not apply to you.
- If you are able to remove the personally identifying elements in your data stream, you may be able to remove yourself from the need to comply with the GDPR.
- If you are able to remove the personally identifiable information, then the regulations will not apply but you must be sure that you have removed the identifiable fields, or obfuscated them in such a way that they can't easily be restored.

What information is covered by the GDPR?

The GDPR covers personal data, that is, any data that uniquely identifies a living person. It also covers data that is listed as "special categories" or that which may be regarded as "sensitive". For example: Ethnic origin, trades union membership or sexual orientation.

Article 4, subsections 1 and 5 state:

(1)-'personal data' means any information relating to an identified or identifiable natural person ('data subject'); an identifiable natural person is one who can be identified, directly or indirectly, in particular by reference to an identifier such as a name, an identification number, location data, an online identifier or to one or more factors specific to the physical, physiological, genetic, mental, economic, cultural or social identity of that natural person;

(5)- 'pseudonymization' means the processing of personal data in such a manner that the personal data can no longer be attributed to a specific data subject without the use of additional information, provided that such additional information is kept separately and is subject to technical and organizational measures to ensure that the personal data are not attributed to an identified or identifiable natural person;

Recital 26 states: *The principles of data protection should apply to any information concerning an identified or identifiable natural person. Personal data which have undergone pseudonymization, which could be attributed to a natural person by the use of additional information should be considered to be information on an identifiable natural person. To determine whether a natural person is identifiable, account should be taken of all the means reasonably likely to be used, such as singling out, either by the controller or by another person to identify the natural person directly or indirectly. To ascertain whether means are reasonably likely to be used to identify the natural person, account should be taken of all objective factors, such as the costs of and the amount of time required for identification, taking into consideration the available technology at the time of the processing and technological developments. The principles of data protection should therefore not apply to anonymous information, namely information which does not relate to an identified or identifiable natural person or to personal data rendered anonymous in such a manner that the data subject is not or no longer identifiable. This Regulation does not therefore concern the processing of such anonymous information, including for statistical or research purposes.*

If you have been able to anonymize (or pseudonymize) your data then you will be exempt from the GDPR but you need to be sure that your data can't be returned to a "normal" state if you are relying on the way that you have obfuscated the personal details. You should seek the advice of a certified GDPR practitioner or a lawyer who is familiar with the workings of the GDPR. The cost of getting it wrong could be very high.

If you are working under the authority of your government and are directed by an act of parliament, then the GDPR may not apply to the data you hold and process. But unless one of the above does apply to your operation, then you will need to meet the requirements of the GDPR.

The GDPR is not just a European issue

The GDPR is EU legislation but it applies to any organization that stores or processes personal data belonging to a citizen of the EU or anyone living within the EU. In theory if you are a rural American organization with a handful of EU citizens as customers the GDPR will apply to your use of and processing of their data. Article 3 of the GDPR states:

1. *This Regulation applies to the processing of personal data in the context of the activities of an establishment of a controller or a processor in the Union, regardless of whether the processing takes place in the Union or not.*
2. *This Regulation applies to the processing of personal data of data subjects who are in the Union by a controller or processor not established in the Union, where the processing activities are related to:*

    (a) *the offering of goods or services, irrespective of whether a payment of the data subject is required, to such data subjects in the Union; or*
    (b) *the monitoring of their behaviour as far as their behaviour takes place within the Union.*

3. *This Regulation applies to the processing of personal data by a controller not established in the Union, but in a place where Member State law applies by virtue of public international law.*

See also Recitals 22, 23, 24 and 25.

If you process the personal data of EU citizens, then you will need to find out which SA you should report a breach to. Assuming that your website is in English, then you may wish to deal with an English speaking SA, in which case you may choose to work with the Data Protection Commissioner in Ireland (www. dataprotection.ie) or the Data Protection Commissioner in the UK (www.ico. org.uk). For non-English speaking countries you may choose to use one of the remaining 26 Commissioners.

Therefore, if you have customers or clients who are EU Citizens you will need to understand how the GDPR applies to your organization.

Can you choose a Supervisory Authority (SA)?

The GDPR was primarily designed to deal with organizations that are resident within the EU but the Regulation recognized that not all processing of EU data subjects will be by companies that reside within the EU. Cyberspace is not as borderless as many would think or even hope, so it is easy to find that you have fallen foul of some legislation in a country where you do not reside but where you are trading.

Article 27 deals with "***Representatives of controllers or processors not established in the Union.***"

It states:

1. *Where Article 3(2) "(This Regulation applies to the processing of personal data of data subjects who are in the Union by a controller or processor not established in the Union, where the processing activities are related to: (a) the offering of goods or services, irrespective of whether a payment of the data subject is required, to such data subjects in the Union)" applies, the controller or the processor shall designate in writing a representative in the Union.*
2. *This obligation shall not apply to:*

    (a) *processing which is occasional, does not include, on a large scale, processing of special categories of data as referred to in Article 9(1) or processing of personal data relating to criminal convictions and offences referred to in Article 10, and is unlikely to result in a risk to the rights and freedoms of natural persons, taking into account the nature, context, scope and purposes of the processing; or*
    (b) *a public authority or body.*

3. *The representative shall be established in one of the Member States where the data subjects, whose personal data are processed in relation to the offering of goods or services to them, or whose behavior is monitored, are.*
4. *The representative shall be mandated by the controller or processor to be addressed in addition to or instead of the controller or the processor by, in particular, supervisory authorities and data subjects, on all issues related to processing, for the purposes of ensuring compliance with this Regulation.*
5. *The designation of a representative by the controller or processor shall be without prejudice to legal actions which could be initiated against the controller or the processor themselves.*

This could be of interest to organizations that are processing significant amounts of data of EU citizens. The important thing to remember is that in the event of a breach that needs to be reported to an SA, it will be better for your organization if you know in advance who to report it to, rather than having various data subjects complaining to their SA and then trying to find out who the Lead SA will be.

To find out which SA is best for your business then details are available here:

http://ec.europa.eu/justice/article-29/structure/data-protection-authorities/index_en.htm

Does the GDPR affect your whole organization?

Unfortunately, it is not possible to give a definitive answer to this question and the rest of this section is solely in the opinion of the authors and is not to be taken as advice, only guidance.

If you are a large, multi-national organization parts of your organization may well be departments, divisions or separate companies that operate outside of the EU and the UK and do not hold or process data relating to the natural persons of, or residing in, the EU/EEA/UK (i.e. the GDPR area). The data that these parts of your organization process may well be governed by other data protection legislation but will almost certainly be outside of the GDPR area of influence. When the data relates to EU/UK citizens or residents, then the data will still be subject to the GDPR and may need separate terms and conditions as well as additional security monitoring.

But there is another type of organization that may be able to structure their data to reduce the impact of the GDPR. This is an organization that mainly deals with non-EU data but has a small proportion of data subjects that are covered by the GDPR and may choose to split their data into GDPR and non-GDPR data. Why would you want to do this? While there are very real benefits to the people protected by the GDPR, there are some potentially large changes to the working practices of the organizations affected by the change. Customers will have to be given a real choice as to whether they are put onto a marketing data base. You will have to assume that they do not want to receive marketing material unless they specifically state that they want to receive it. You will then have to record the fact that you have their clear and unambiguous permission and when this was given. The list of data subjects that have agreed to be marketed will have to be available to an auditor, as will other evidence that you are complying with the GDPR. If a GDPR protected customer submits a subject access request, you must respond within one month unless it is a complex process. Article 12 subsection 3 states:

The controller shall provide information on action taken on a request under Articles 15 to 22 to the data subject without undue delay and in any event within one month of receipt of the request. That period may be extended by two further months where necessary, taking into account the complexity and number of the requests. The controller shall inform the data subject of any such extension within one month of receipt of the request, together with the reasons for the delay. Where the data subject makes the request by electronic form means, the information shall be provided by electronic means where possible, unless otherwise requested by the data subject.

You may not have to provide this facility to your customers that are outside of the GDPR protection or you may choose to charge them.

Pan-national data

It seems obvious that a multi-national company operating in a non-European country that has suffered a data breach in, for example, Nigeria, where the data that had been compromised relates to the natural living people of that country, would be unlikely to face a regulatory fine from a Supervisory Authority (SA) in a country that was under the jurisdiction of the GDPR.

However, that company may have placed its data in a cloud environment where GDPR-protected data belonging to a European based subsidiary was next to it. In this scenario, as long as the GDPR protected data was not compromised, then the

Nigerian company should not face a regulatory fine from a SA within the GDPR area. But what if adjacent GDPR-protected data were compromised? – Would the Nigerian company face an investigation from the same SA? The answer is that the organization will be investigated by the SA for the data that is under the "jurisdiction" of the GDPR. They will have had to comply with a number of regulators depending upon where the data originated or was collected from and if the data resides in a single cloud-based data warehouse, then the organization may well have to operate so that they comply with the strictest data protection regime in the countries that they operate in.

Now, it *may* be possible to split your data into GDPR-protected and non-GDPR data. Why would you want to do this? There are two reasons: first, your traditional method of trading may have relied on practices that the GDPR is now forcing you to change. You may use marketing that is opt-in by default, you may wish to sell your customer data without asking your customers for permission, or you may, in short, be processing data in a way that is acceptable to the majority of your customers but not the customers that fall under the GDPR. So, you face a choice and you must either change your working practices and procedures in order to comply with the requirements of the GDPR or you need to split your data into GDPR and non-GDPR-protected data.

Another reason is that in the event of a regulatory fine being levied, one element that is used to determine the size of the fine is the volume of data that has been compromised. If you have suffered a data breach and some of your data subjects are protected by the GDPR, and you do not know which they are, then you will have to report the breach as if all of the data subjects are protected by the GDPR. This will increase the size of the "problem" and may well result in an increased fine.

Here are some examples that demonstrate the above points:

Example 1

Organization A is a successful and rapidly expanding company that operates out of offices in Cookeville, Tennessee, USA. They have been selling software products within America for several years and are growing at a steady pace. Their products are unique and popular and they expand by selling to their existing customers as well as acquiring new ones. They are looking to actively expand into Europe by running an advertising campaign. However, before they do they want to under-stand the impact of the GDPR on their business model.

By analysing the data that they hold they find that under 5% of their existing customers are likely to live in Europe. These are then split away from their main customers and placed in a separate data silo. They then create a new website that will identify the incoming IP address of a customer and either send them to the GDPR-protected site or to the American one. The GDPR site has an updated privacy policy and uses an opt-out for marketing by default as well as displaying enhanced rights for their data subjects. They find that most of their customers don't bother to tick the marketing box, whereas on the American site, most do not bother to remove the tick that has been pre-placed in the marketing box. The result is that the majority of the American customers can be marketed but only a small number of the GDPR-protected customers can.

In addition, when they buy a mailing list of American consumers, the price is considerably lower than the same size list that contains GDPR-protected data subjects. This is because American companies are able to harvest their customers based on user apathy. Most customers visiting American sites will leave their consent pre-ticked and within the terms and conditions of these sites will be the statements that the company passes their personal data to outside organizations. Within the GDPR regulated websites the practice is not allowed. Consent must have been clearly and explicitly given, so most customers will not bother to give consent for the company to market them and fewer still will give permission for the company to sell their personal data.

By taking the trouble to identify the GDPR regulated customers the company is able to operate within the rules as laid down by the GDPR without having to change their complete working practices. The GDPR customers will be retained for less time if they no longer buy products, as defined by the company retention policy in their privacy statement. On the American site there is no mention of the fact that customers, once registered, will be retained indefinitely. Only the customers who bother to unsubscribe from a mail-shot will be removed from the mailing list.

Example 2

A UK based company has been selling used baby-clothes by mail-order to young parents, mainly mothers, for several years. The company has found that this re-sale of goods is very popular because, as young babies grow rapidly, the clothes that they buy and sell are always in good condition (their quality control is very important) and very competitively priced. However, they will need to update their policies to reflect the fact that their customers must ask to be marketed. Most of their customers are happy to receive information but they tend not to bother to give explicit consent, so the mailing list is hard to grow. They can only gain new customers for proactive marketing when a young parent visits the website and opts to receive mail-shots. The company has improved their success rate slightly by offering new customers a discount voucher if they will accept the marketing emails. Because of the specialist nature of their business, however, they are unable to buy general mailing lists because the success rate will be extremely low if they try to market to the general population.

The company then decides to expand into Japan where UK baby-clothes are becoming very popular with young families. They find that the number of mailing lists available in Japan is high and the cost is very reasonable due to the fact that it is easy for marketing companies to build up their lists.

(e)   *kept in a form which permits identification of data subjects for no longer than is necessary for the purposes for which the personal data are processed; personal data may be stored for longer periods insofar as the personal data will be processed solely for archiving purposes in the public interest, scientific or historical research purposes or statistical purposes ... subject to implementation of the appropriate technical and organizational measures required by the GDPR in order to safeguard the rights and freedoms of individuals;*

(f)   *processed in a manner that ensures appropriate security of the personal data, including protection against unauthorized or unlawful processing and against accidental loss, destruction or damage, using appropriate technical or organizational measures.*

Article 5(2) requires that "the controller shall be responsible for, and be able to demonstrate, compliance with the principles."

Lawfulness of processing conditions 6(1)(a) – Consent of the data subject 6(1)(b) – Processing is necessary for the performance of a contract with the data subject or "to take steps to enter into a contract";

6(1)(c) – processing is necessary for compliance with a legal obligation

6(1)(d) – processing is necessary to protect the vital interests of a data subject or another person

6(1)(e) – processing is necessary for the performance of a task carried out in the public interest or in the exercise of official authority vested in the controller

6(1)(f) – processing is necessary for the purposes of legitimate interests pursued by the controller or a third party, except where such interests are overridden by the interests, rights or freedoms of the data subject and in particular where the data subject is a child.

Note that this condition is not available to processing carried out by public authorities in the performance of their tasks.

Conditions for processing special categories of data:

9(2)(a) – Explicit consent of the data subject, unless reliance on consent is prohibited by EU or Member State law.

9(2)(b) – Processing is necessary for carrying out obligations under employment, social security or social protection law, or a collective agreement.

9(2)(c) – Processing is necessary to protect the vital interests of a data subject or another individual where the data subject is physically or legally incapable of giving consent.

9(2)(d) – Processing carried out by a not-for-profit body with a political, philosophical, religious or trade union aim provided the processing relates only to members or former members (or those who have regular contact with it in connection with those purposes) and provided there is no disclosure to a third party without consent.

9(2)(e) – Processing relates to personal data manifestly made public by the data subject.

9(2)(f) – Processing is necessary for the establishment, exercise or defence of legal claims or whenever courts are acting in their judicial capacity.

9(2)(g) – Processing is necessary for reasons of substantial public interest, on the basis of Union or Member State law which is proportionate to the aim pursued and which contains appropriate safeguards.

9(2)(h) – Processing is necessary for the purposes of preventive or occupational medicine, for the assessment of the working capacity of the employee, medical diagnosis, the provision of health or social care or treatment or management of health or social care systems and services on the basis of Union or Member State law or a contract with a health professional.

9(2)(i) – Processing is necessary for reasons of public interest in the area of public health, such as protecting against serious cross-border threats to health or ensuring high standards of healthcare and of medicinal products or medical devices.

9(2)(j) – Processing is necessary for archiving purposes in the public interest, or scientific and historical research purposes or statistical purposes in accordance with Article 89(1).

Consent

Consent under the GDPR must be a freely given, specific, informed and unambiguous indication of the individual's wishes. There must be some form of clear affirmative action – or in other words, a positive opt-in – consent cannot be inferred from silence, pre-ticked boxes or inactivity. Consent must also be separate from other terms and conditions, and you will need to provide simple ways for people to withdraw consent. Public authorities and employers will need to take particular care to ensure that consent is freely given. Consent has to be verifiable, and individuals generally have more rights where you rely on consent to process their data.

Please note – it may seem common sense to have the permission of the data subject and it would therefore be reasonable to assume that "Consent" is the preferred lawful basis for processing but this is not the case. Consent may be given and then refused and if this happens, you will not be able to process the data. It is often better to have an alternative legal basis for processing and many companies will be using consent as a last resort.

However, while you do not need consent in order to process, there may be some aspects of your operation that you will need consent for. In particular you must have consent if you are going to market an individual, so make sure you understand the difference between general processing, like order processing or running an on-line account and marketing.

Remember that you can rely on other lawful bases apart from consent – for example, where processing is necessary for the purposes of your organization's or a third party's legitimate interest.

You are not required to automatically "repaper" or refresh all existing DPA consents in preparation for the GDPR. But if you rely on individuals' consent to process their data, make sure it will meet the GDPR standard on being specific, granular, clear, prominent, opt-in, properly documented and easily withdrawn. If not, alter your consent mechanisms and seek fresh GDPR-compliant consent, or find an alternative to consent.

Section

3

Key roles

There are a number of key roles referred to in the Regulation and it is important that you understand how they differ from one another. The various terms will be used throughout this book but here are the definitions.

Data Protection Officer (DPO)

Under the GDPR it is necessary to appoint a DPO in three specific cases. These are:

1. where the processing is carried out by a public authority or body;
2. where the core activities of the controller or the processor consist of processing operations, which require regular and systematic monitoring of data subjects on a large scale; or
3. where the core activities of the controller or the processor consist of processing on a large scale of special categories of data or personal data relating to criminal convictions and offences.

The GDPR does not define "large scale" but does offer some guidance in a document that was issued by the WP29 Working Party:

The GDPR does not define what constitutes large-scale. The WP29 recommends that the following factors, in particular, be considered when determining whether the processing is carried out on a large scale:

*   *The number of data subjects concerned – either as a specific number or as a proportion of the relevant population*
*   *The volume of data and/or the range of different data items being processed*

- *The duration, or permanence, of the data processing activity*
- *The geographical extent of the processing activity*

However, if you believe that you are processing large amounts of data or data for large numbers of people, it will be wise to consider whether you need to appoint a DPO.

If you are sure that you do not meet the threshold now but are likely to in the reasonably near future, you may wish to appoint a DPO.

While this will be another function that your company will need to allow for, the DPO does not have to be a dedicated or full-time employee. It can be an existing employee so long as they have enough time and independence to perform their job well.

If you need a DPO, you don't have to have a dedicated member of staff, you can share this task with other organizations and there will probably be a number of security consultancies that will be offering this service; but beware of "outsourcing" your responsibilities.

The role of the Data Protection Officer

The DPO is responsible for:

1. Advising the controller and/or processor of their responsibilities and ensuring that they are being adhered to.
2. Monitoring compliance with the GDPR and ensuring that the organization is meeting its obligations. Where they are working with a number of different countries within the EU, they will need to ensure that they meet all the requirements.
3. Providing advice within their organization on the data protection impact assessment (DPIA) as specified in Article 35.
4. Cooperating with your or any other supervisory authority.
5. Acting as a contact point for your or any other supervisory authority.

When the DPO is working for an organization that is subject to (or subject in part to) the GDPR, it can be more straightforward if you are processing within the EU and therefore under the jurisdiction of a nominated SA. If your processing and data are completely outside of the EU and you suffer a breach that requires reporting then you will have to decide which SA to report the breach to. This may depend upon where the majority of your customers reside or are citizens of and you should seek legal advice.

If you appoint a DPO then Article 38, subsection 3 states that they must report directly to the highest management level. How you arrange their reporting structure will depend on the nature, size and complexity of your organization but you will need to consider this requirement. However, they must be allowed to operate independently, they may not be dismissed for performing their duties and they must be given the resources to carry out the function of DPO.

For smaller organizations it may be practical to share a DPO between several organizations or to use the services of a specialist contractor.

Data controller

According to the GDPR a data controller is defined thus:

> 'controller' means the natural or legal person, public authority, agency or other body which, alone or jointly with others, determines the purposes and means of the processing of personal data; where the purposes and means of such processing are determined by Union or Member State law, the controller or the specific criteria for its nomination may be provided for by Union or Member State law; (GDPR Article 4(7))

The Information Commissioner defines a data controller thus:

> "Data controller" means a person who (either alone or jointly or in common with other persons) determines the purposes for which and the manner in which any personal data are, or are to be processed

In the article "Data controllers and processors 20140506 version 1.0" the Information Commissioner then goes on to explain that there can be confusion as to whether you are a processor or a controller and says:

If all parties are working well together to make sure that compliance issues such as giving subject access or keeping personal data secure are addressed, then the question of data protection responsibility may seem academic. However, the distinction between a data controller and data processor can have significant real-world consequences. For example, if there is a data breach it is essential for both the organizations involved and the ICO to be able to determine where responsibility lies.

This can be difficult, and there is evidence of confusion on the part of some organizations as to their respective roles and therefore their data protection responsibilities. It is important that the various organizations involved in a data processing activity establish their roles and responsibilities at an early stage, particularly before the processing commences. This will help to ensure that there are no gaps in organizations' responsibilities – such gaps could result in subject access requests going unanswered, for example.

How to determine whether an organization is a data controller or a data processor

The data controller determines the purposes for which and the manner in which personal data is processed. It can do this either on its own or jointly or in common with other organizations. This means that the data controller exercises overall control over the "why" and the "how" of a data processing activity. The definition provides flexibility, for example it can allow one data controller to mainly, but **not exclusively,** control the purpose of the processing with another data controller. It can also allow another data controller to have some say in determining the purpose whilst being mainly responsible for controlling the manner of the processing. Many business relationships work this way.

To determine whether you are a data controller you need to ascertain which organization decides:

- to collect the personal data in the first place and the legal basis for doing so;
- which items of personal data to collect, i.e. the content of the data;
- the purpose or purposes the data are to be used for;
- which individuals to collect data about;
- whether to disclose the data, and if so, who to;
- whether subject access and other individuals' rights apply i.e. the application of exemptions; and
- how long to retain the data or whether to make non-routine amendments to the data.

These are all decisions that can only be taken by the data controller as part of its overall control of the data processing operation.

The above advice was provided by the Information Commissioner as part of a guide to the Data Protection Act 1998 but the definition holds true for the GDPR as well.

There are important differences between the roles as far as the regulation is concerned and we would advise you to read further if you have any doubts as to whether your particular activity makes you a controller or processor.

Data processor

The GDPR states:

> 'Data processor' means a natural or legal person, public authority, agency or other body which processes personal data on behalf of the controller;

In the publication "Data controllers and data processors – 20140506" the Information Commissioner states:

"Data processor" in relation to personal data, means any person (other than an employee of the data controller) who processes the data on behalf of the data controller.

"Processing" in relation to information or data means obtaining, recording or holding the information or data or carrying out any operation or set of operations on the information or data, including —

a) *Organization, adaptation or alteration of the information or data,*
b) *Retrieval, consultation or use of the information or data,*
c) *Disclosure of the information or data by transmission, dissemination or otherwise making available, or*
d) *Alignment, combination, blocking, erasure or destruction of the information or data.*

The definition of processing can be useful in determining the sort of activities an organization can engage in and what decisions it can take within its role as a data processor. The definition of "processing" suggests that a data processor's activities must be limited to the more "technical" aspects of an operation, such as data storage, retrieval or erasure. Activities such as interpretation, the exercise of professional judgement or significant decision-making in relation to personal data must be carried out by a data controller. This is not a hard and fast distinction and some aspects of "processing", for example "holding" personal data, could be common to the controller and the processor.

Some organizations will have more complex forms of processing and if you are in any doubt you should seek the advice of a Certified GDPR Practitioner to be certain. However, for the vast majority of organizations it will be clear if they are acting as a Controller (and controlling the data and making decisions about the retention policy, the legality of processing the data etc.) or working in a subordinate role of Processor.

Sub-processor

When we look at sub-contractors, then it can be difficult to see whether the sub-processor is a controller or a processor. In the UK, the ICO guidance states:

There can be a tendency for the 'main' data controller organization to deem its sub-contractor, professional adviser or consultant to be its data processor. Sometimes this can be written into a contract. However, the fact that an organization contracts or employs another organization to provide a service to it does not mean that the other organization becomes its data processor in every case. Whether an organization is a data controller or data processor will depend on their role and responsibilities in relation to the processing.

Organizations often use a professional or business service to obtain specialist assistance, for example:

- *a lawyer to provide legal advice;*
- *an accountant to provide accountancy services;*
- *a doctor to provide a medical report on an individual in connection with an insurance claim;*
- *a recruitment agency to recruit specialist staff for an engineering firm; or*
- *a counselling service to assist traumatized individuals employed by the emergency services.*

In these cases, the client will not have sole data controller responsibility even though they initiated the work by asking for advice or commissioning a report. Responsibility also lies with the professional service provider itself because it determines what information to obtain and process in order to do the work and because it is answerable itself for the content. The use of a lawyer provides a good illustration of why providers of professional services are not usually just data processors. A client receives legal advice and, regardless of whether or not he chooses to follow the advice, would not ask the lawyer to make amendments to the original advice – the lawyer controls the detailed content of the advice. Lawyers would also have their own professional responsibilities in terms of record keeping, the confidentiality of communications and so forth. Again, this points towards lawyers and similar professional service providers being data controllers in their own right.

The ICO then gives a number of examples and these can be helpful to understand the difference between the roles and also to see why there is confusion. We give three here.

Examples

Payment services

An on-line retailer works in co-operation with a third-party payment company to process customers' transactions. The payment company is not the retailer's data processor, even though there is a contract in place between the two companies that covers areas such as service standards and financial arrangements. This is because the payment company:

- *Decides which information it needs from customers in order to process their payments correctly;*
- *Exercises control over the other purposes the customer's data is used for, for example direct marketing;*
- *Has legal requirements of its own to meet, for example relating to the use and retention of payment card data; and*
- *Has its own terms and conditions that apply directly to the retailer's customers.*

Therefore, the payment service is a data controller in its own right and will have full data protection responsibility for the processing it carries out.

IT service providers

A car hire company contracts a vehicle-tracking company to install devices in its cars and monitor them so that cars can be recovered if they go missing. They specify that the tracking company should track all the company's cars and send back the location data to the hire company six hours after the end of the hire period if the car has not been returned.

However, despite these instructions, the vehicle-tracking company is a data controller in its own right. This is because it has sufficient freedom to use its expertise to decide which information to collect about cars (and their drivers) and how to analyze this. It is entirely in control of its own data collection – the operation of the vehicle-tracking software is a trade secret and the hire company does not even know what information is collected. Although the hire company determines the overall purpose of the tracking (the recovery of its cars), the fact that the tracking company has such a degree of freedom to decide which information to collect and how, means it is a data controller in its own right.

The above examples were taken from the ICO Guidance on Data Controllers and Data Processors.

Section

4

Rights of the data subject

Because the subject of "rights" is a key element of the GDPR we look at the various rights in some detail. Many other information protection laws deal with the way that data is to be protected and what to do in the event of a breach of security but the rights of individuals are often overlooked.

Many of these "rights" will need to be made clear in the form of a Privacy Notice.

Within the GDPR, Chapter III deals with these rights and runs from Article 12 through to Article 23. In addition, Article 34 deals with the notification of a data breach to the individual and so we include it in this section. We provide a summary of these Articles here.

The right to be informed

Article 13 states that you are required to tell your data subjects certain things depending upon where you collected the data. For data that was collected from the data subject you must tell them:

a) the identity and contact details of the data controller and, if appropriate, the data controller's representative;

b) the contact details of the data protection officer if one has been appointed;

c) the purpose of the processing and the legal basis for the processing. This should be specific and not a vague generalization.

d) where the processing is based on a claim of "the legitimate interest" of the controller or a third-party;

e) the categories of recipients of the personal data.

At the time when the data was obtained you must tell the data subject:

a) the length of time that you will store the data;
b) that she/he has the right to have any errors corrected or to have the data erased or to restrict processing of the data;
c) they have the "right of data portability". That means they have the right to request a copy of their data in a common format;
d) when the data subject has given consent for the processing of their data for one or more specific purposes, they have the right to withdraw their consent at any time;they have the right to lodge a complaint with a SA but remember that if you are processing and storing your data outside of the EU, they may be able to choose the SA that they complain to, based on where they live;
e) whether you are processing their data based on a statutory or a contractual basis;
f) whether you use automated decision making including profiling and you may also need to give them meaningful information about the logic involved in the decisions;
g) when and how you intend to further process the data;
h) the above does not apply if the data subject already has the information.

So, this is where your Privacy Notice needs to contain the legal basis for your collection and processing as well as the details listed above.

Article 14 states that for data that was not obtained from the data subject you should tell them:

a) where the data was obtained;
b) the contact details of the data protection officer if one has been appointed;
c) the purpose of the processing and the legal basis for the processing. This should be specific and not a vague generalization;
d) where the processing is based on a claim of "the legitimate interest" of the controller or a third-party;
e) the categories of recipients of the personal data;
f) the categories of recipients of the personal data;
g) if you intend to transfer the data to a country outside of the EU also tell them if the Commission has decided that the country or organization in question has adequate safeguards in place to protect the data.

In addition to the above, you must tell them:

a) how long you will retain the data;
b) where the processing is based;
c) the fact that they may request access to, error correction and deletion of the data or to restrict processing;
d) that they may have the right to withdraw their consent at any time;
e) the right to lodge a complaint with a SA;

f)   from which source the data originated and whether the source was public;
g)   the existence of any automated decision-making including profiling and you may need to tell them the logic involved in the decision making (see Article 22);
h)   where you send data outside of the EU, or to an international organization you need to tell the data subject what safeguards are in place to protect the data
i)   you must provide a copy of the data if requested;
j)   if further copies are requested, you may charge a reasonable fee for them.

You should give the data subjects the above information in a timely manner and a good way of doing this is by using a privacy notice. You should bring this to their attention at the time of collection. While most websites and apps will collect data, many will not specify what they collect and how long it is retained. Under the GDPR this must change and for the data subjects that are under the protection of the Regulation you will need to ensure that they are informed about the above factors.

The right of access

Article 15 deals with the right of access for the data subject. She or he has the right to obtain from the controller the following details relating to their personal data:

a)   the purpose of the processing;
b)   the categories of data;
c)   the recipients or categories of recipient to whom their data will be disclosed;
d)   where possible the amount of time that the data will be retained and if not, the criteria used to determine the time;
e)   the existence of the data subject's right to rectification, erasure, restriction of processing or to object to such processing;
f)   the right to lodge a complaint to a SA;
g)   where the data has not come from the data subject, the source of the data;
h)   the existence of any automated decision-making and meaningful information about the logic used in the automated processing.

1.   Where the data is transferred to a third country or an international organization the data subject must be told what safeguards are in place to protect the data.
2.   You must provide a copy of the data that is being processed. Any further copies may be charged for at a "reasonable fee" based on administrative costs.
3.   The right to obtain a copy referred to in (3) above shall not affect the rights and freedoms of others.

This means that you must tell your customers who to contact if they wish to know what data you have collected and how long you plan to retain it for.

The right to rectification

Article 16 deals with the data subject's right to the rectification of their data. You must allow for the correction of inaccurate data and also to add to any incomplete data. If you have passed on the data you will need to know who you have sent it to and to correct their copy. Corrections and additions to the data must be undertaken without "undue delay" and this is generally taken to mean within one month.

The right to erasure

This is in Article 17 and is also known as "the right to be forgotten". There are three parts to this right.

The data subject shall have the right to have personal data erased where one of the following applies:

a) the personal data is no longer necessary for the purpose for which it was originally collected
b) the data subject withdraws consent to the processing
c) the personal data has been unlawfully processed
d) the personal data has to be erased in order to comply with a legal request
e) the personal data was collected in relation to an offer made to a child. The offer is only lawful if the child is over 16 years old or has been approved by an adult with parental responsibility.

Where the data controller has made the data public and is obliged to erase the data (as above), the controller, taking into account available technology and the cost of implementation, shall take reasonable steps to inform data controllers who are processing the data that the data subject has requested the erasure of their data, along with any links to or copies of the data.

The above two paragraphs (and their subsections) shall not apply if the processing is necessary:

a) for exercising the right to freedom of expression
b) for compliance with a legal obligation
c) for reasons of public interest in the area of health (such as tracking the spread of an epidemic)
d) for archiving purposes in the public interest
e) for the establishment or defence of a legal claim.

The right to restriction of processing

Article 18 deals with the right to restrict processing and says that:

1. The data subject has the right to obtain from the controller restriction of processing where one of the following applies:

    a) The accuracy of the data is in doubt, the restriction will apply for long enough to allow the data controller to verify the accuracy of the data.
    b) The processing is unlawful and the data subject opposes the deletion of the data and requires the processing to be restricted instead.
    c) The controller no longer needs the data for processing but they are required by the data subject to restrict processing for the establishment, exercise or defence of legal claims.
    d) The data subject has the right to object to processing on the basis of their claim that processing is unlawful (see Article 21(1)).

2. Where processing has been restricted based on the above reasons, the data shall, with the exception of storage, only be processed with the data subject's consent or for the establishment, exercise or defence of a legal claim.
3. The data subject who has obtained a restriction of processing shall be informed by the controller before the restriction is lifted.

This is a major change from most previous data protection legislation and may mean an update to your working practices for your customers that fall under the rights of the GDPR. You will need to plan how you will deal with any requests to restrict processing and how you will be able to remove these records from your normal processing.

Obligations relating to rectification, erasure or restriction

Article 19 states that the controller must communicate any rectification, or erasure of personal data or the restriction of processing as above, to each recipient of the data unless this proves impossible or involves a disproportionate effort.

The right to data portability

Article 20 deals with data portability. While this right may need careful planning, it is not open to every data subject. Please read this section to see if you need to be prepared to cater for these requests.

The data subject will have the right to receive a copy of their personal data which they have provided to you in a structured, commonly used and machine-readable format and they have the right to request you to transmit the information to another data controller where:

a) the legal basis for processing the data was "consent", see Article 6(1) point (a) and
b) the processing is carried out by automated means.

1. When this right applies the data subject will be able to request that you transmit the data directly to a data controller of her or his choice provided this is technically feasible.
2. This right is without prejudice to her or his right to have the data erased as in Article 17.
3. This right shall not affect the rights or freedoms of other individuals.

The right to object

Article 21 relates to the right of the data subject to object in a number of situations: if your legal basis for processing is based on Article 6(1) points (e) or (f), i.e. processing is necessary for the performance of a task carried out in the public interest OR processing is necessary for the purpose of the legitimate interest of the controller or a third party (this is an abridged explanation, see Article 6 for full details). Or if you are undertaking profiling, the data subject has the right to object and you may no longer process the data unless you can demonstrate compelling legitimate grounds which override the rights of the complainant or for the establishment, exercise or defence of a legal claim.

1. Where the processing relates to marketing the data subject has the right to object at any time to the processing including profiling.
2. Where the data subject objects to processing for marketing, the processing must stop.
3. As soon as you hear from the data subject, his or her rights under paragraphs 1 and 2 above, shall be brought to their attention and must be separate from any other information.
4. In the context of the use of information society services, and notwithstanding directive 2002/58/EC (the ePrivacy Directive) the data subject may object by automated means using technical specification.
5. Where personal data are used for scientific or historical research or for statistical purposes relating to Article 89(1) then the data subject, on the grounds relating to his or her particular situation, shall have the right to object the processing of their personal data unless the processing is carried out for public interest reasons.

This will need careful thought to avoid a major impact on the rest of your customers.

Automated individual decision-making including profiling

Article 22 deals with automated decision-making and states:

1. *The data subject has the right not to be subject to a decision based solely on automated processing including profiling which produces legal effects or similarly significant effects on her or him.*

2.   *Paragraph 1 shall not apply if the decision:*

    (a)   *is necessary for entering into, or the performance of a contract between the data subject and the data controller*

    (b)   *is authorized by Union or Member State law to which the controller is subject and which contains measures to safeguard the rights of the data subject*

    (c)   *is based on the data subject's explicit consent.*

3.   *In the cases referred to in points (a) and (c) above the data controller shall implement suitable measures to safeguard the rights and freedoms of the data subject at least the right to obtain human intervention from the controller to express his or her point of view to contest the decision.*

4.   *Decisions referred to paragraph 2 shall not be based on special categories of data, as in Article 9(1) unless point (a) or (g) of Article 9(2) applies and there are suitable measures in place to safeguard the data subject's rights.*

Restrictions

Article 23 deals with restrictions to the above, based on a proportionate measure to protect national security or other legal issues. Please see the full list of restriction that apply in Article 23 but as these will not apply to the vast majority of commercial organizations, we have not listed them here.

Privacy notices

Within the GDPR you will not find the term "Privacy Notice" but starting with Article 13 above you will see the information that needs to be contained in your privacy notices.

Please note that we say notices, plural because you need to tell your customers what you collect, why you collect it, how long you will retain it, who you share it with and how they can contact you to obtain the details of the above. However, you must do this "in plain English", or whatever language you are operating in. Simply providing all the information in one vast tome will not satisfy the GDPR.

If you have ever tried to read a privacy notice from any of the world's large writers of operating systems, search engines or social media organizations you will see that while they are 100% accurate, they are also of limited practical value to a member of the general public.

Your privacy notice must be written clearly and able to be understood by your intended customers. So, if you are designing an application that is aimed at children, then your privacy notice must be able to be understood by a child and only contain the language that they will be familiar with.

The best option is to provide a privacy notice that relates to the information you are collecting at that point. So, if you have a customer who is opening an account, say to use your website, then look at the fields that you are asking them to fill in and explain why you need it, what you will do with it and how long you will retain it for. Simple and concise language. If you do this, you may well have many privacy notices but each one will be short, clear and easy to understand in the context of what you are collecting.

There are many examples of good and bad privacy notices and a search will show you a number. The ICO has a number of free-to-use resources that will guide you (see www.ico.org.uk and use their search facility to look at examples of privacy notices) and if you are a member of a trade body you may find that they will have examples of good practice that is specific to your area of operation.

Section

5

Your GDPR project

GDPR tools

Before you start your GDPR project you may be familiar with or wish to use some tools to assist you. Indeed, there are a number of GDPR tools available and whilst they will not do the job for you, they will undoubtedly help.

Microsoft's GDPR Assessment tool is a quick, on-line, self-evaluation tool available at no cost. It helps your organization review its overall level of readiness to comply with the GDPR. The Microsoft GDPR Detailed Assessment can tell organizations where they are on their journey to GDPR readiness.

SNOW GDPR Risk Assessment's tool provides complete visibility of all devices, users, and applications across on-premises, cloud, and mobile environments. The purpose of this tool is to help build an effective GDPR plan and response. Automated discovery provides a detailed account of which users have access to which applications and cloud services.

Nymity's Compliance toolkit identifies 39 articles in the GDPR that need evidence to demonstrate compliance. This toolkit equips privacy officers with the resources necessary to achieve demonstrable compliance. Some resources within the toolkit are assessment questions, an accountability roadmap, and the Nymity Privacy Management Accountability Framework (adapted for the GDPR).

Totalprogramme control offers a simple on-line self-assessment that can be used for your own organization or for a supplier and gives a graphical representation of your compliance.

Using tools such as these will give you a solid audit trail of your project and may assist if your compliance is challenged.

GDPR: a breakdown

As explained in previous sections, the GDPR is extensive and exacting on how you should comply. The reality is that you will need to balance your approach between ultimate alignment with every detail within the GDPR and the realities of running your business; so here is a reality check. The GDPR consists of 99 Articles and 173 Recitals. The Recitals are designed to give clarity to the various Articles. If you are tracking a compliance project you won't need all 99 Articles, so here is how they are grouped.

Articles 1–4 deal with general provisions; you should be aware of these but they will not affect how you comply. For example, Article 4 deals with the 26 definitions used within the various Articles, so you need to be aware of what the definitions are, but they will not materially affect how you approach the project. Please see Article 3, "Territorial Scope" and Article 27 which you will need to take into account if you are located outside of the EU.

Articles 5–11 deal with the principles and it is important that you check that you are abiding by these.

Articles 12–23 deal with the rights of the data subjects; you must ensure that you have these embedded in your working practices and make any changes that you deem necessary.

Articles 24–39 relate to controllers and processors. You will need to ensure that your project team understand how your organization is working. Are you a data controller, data processor or both, do you need a data protection officer? The answers to these will be in this section so you will need to understand the responsibilities and liabilities that you have and how this will affect your day-to-day processes and procedures.

Articles 40–43 deal with codes of conduct and certification, which is mainly an administrative process.

Articles 44–50 cover transfers of personal data to third countries and international organizations. If you and anyone that you send personal data to only work within the EU, then this section will not affect your compliance project. If you do transfer personal data outside of the EU, then Article 47, which deals with binding corporate rules will be of great interest and you should understand what this means for your organization.

Articles 51–59 deal with the supervisory authorities and how they operate. This is important but does not have any impact on how to achieve and maintain your compliance with the GDPR.

Articles 60–76 are administrative articles and deal with how the EU will deal with cooperation and consistency throughout the Member States. These Articles will not affect how you run your GDPR project(s).

Articles 77–91 cover the various remedies, liability and penalties that matter if there is a breach and also deal with provisions relating to specific processing situations. For example, Article 88 offers EU Union Member States additional protection for employees, so while this may affect you in the future, it will not alter the way that you are planning to achieve compliance.

Finally, **Articles 92–99** are mainly administrative rules.

We can see that from the original 99 Articles, your compliance project(s) will mainly be working with Articles 1–39 if you and your suppliers operate solely within the EU and Articles 1–39 and 44–50 if you are an international organization. We can now look at your GDPR project from a purely compliance point of view. As compliance is based on ensuring that the personal data you hold is justified, accurate and secure, your project will be designed to work with the various data streams that you have. This means that your project will likely be broken down into the following typical five phases:

Phase 1 – Allocate a project team representative from each data owner, for example HR, Accounts, Sales and Marketing; your various production departments will have representatives in the overall project. This is where you may well form a number of smaller project teams so that each data owner can examine the data that they process and store and ensure that they have a valid business need to retain each of the fields. They will also need to confirm that their existing data retention rules are consistent with and can be justified within the provisions of the GDPR. Within this work stream, each project team will need to perform a Data Protection Impact Assessment (DPIA), or a Privacy Impact Assessment (PIA) in the UK. This phase will include a risk assessment and reduction process to ensure that your various data sources have been assessed on a business basis and that you have looked at your suppliers who hold or process the personal data that you are responsible for. You should now be compliant with **Articles 1, 2, 3, 4, 5, (8, 9 part), 11, 14, 35** and **36.**

Phase 2 – Understand how you are operating. Are you a data controller or processor or both? How do you control your suppliers and ensure that they will be compliant? If you are a public authority or if processing operations require regular and systematic monitoring or data subjects on a large scale or processing of special categories of data, you will need a data protection officer (DPO). The meaning of special categories of personal data is explained in Articles 9, 10 and the role of the DPO is explained in Articles 37–39. If a DPO is needed you should recruit one or ensure that you have a contract in place if this is a position that you will be sharing with another organization. This will ensure that you are compliant with **Articles 24, 25, 26, 27, 28, 29, 30, 31, 37, 38** and **39.**

Phase 3 – A company-wide awareness programme to make sure that any working practices have been updated to ensure that all employees understand that the company is fully committed to complying with the GDPR, what this means in terms of how you communicate with your data subjects, how and where you display your Privacy Notices and how you comply with Subject Access Requests. At this stage you should be compliant with **Articles 6, 7, (8, 9 from Phase 1 above), 10, 11, 12, 13, 14** and **15.**

Phase 4 – If you are the data controller, this is where you will focus on your processes for rectifying any inaccurate data that you become aware of and how you deal with an erasure request (i.e. the right to be forgotten), from a data subject, or how you will deal with these requests from the data controller if you are the data processor. This will make you comply with **Article 16.**

Phase 5 – This focuses on your business applications and the IT systems that support them. You must ensure that your systems are able to comply with the right to erasure (above), and if your applications need to be updated then this has been arranged and the necessary testing and sign-off within the agreed time-scales has been achieved in order to meet your project obligations. You may also need to be able to comply with a data portability request, as well as ensuring that you adopt Security by Design at the heart of your IT system design. You must ensure that your existing security testing processes (penetration testing of your perimeter defences and perhaps meeting your payment card industry obligations) have been updated. This stage will include your ability to identify a security breach and how you will notify the authorities. You may need to update your internal monitoring and reporting procedures. You will now comply with **Articles 17, 18, 19, 20, 21, 22, 23 (if applicable) 32, 33** and **34.**

These five phases will ensure that you have complied with the key requirements of the GDPR. As well as complying you will need to retain the necessary documentation so that you can satisfy an audit of your compliance. In this section we will break the project down into smaller phases but the process of complying will be the same.

This is a business project, not just IT

Many companies see data protection as something that "IT does" and while it is true that your IT team will have input into the GDPR project, you will need input and resource from every department that collects, uses or stores personal data that is covered by the GDPR. As you progress through the project you will see that your retention policy, your ability to identify all the data fields that you hold, and your ability to know exactly what data your suppliers hold will be critical to the success of your project. Your IT team will be able to help with this information but they should not be making business decisions on your behalf.

You will need Board commitment

This is likely to be a project that needs significant resource and it will need to be a high priority if you are to avoid the possibility of a legal challenge. If you do suffer a breach before you are compliant, then your ability to demonstrate that you have made good progress with a fully funded project that has the commitment of the executive of your company will be vital. You will also need to be able to provide "proof" of your progress, so maintaining a good audit trail of the progress of the project is extremely important. Your DPO should provide regular updates to the Board directly or through your Audit and Risk Committee (or equivalent).

You should have an Executive Champion

You should have an Executive Champion who will be responsible for liaising with the Board. It is this person who will fight for your resource and explain what progress you are making. They will not necessarily need to be working full time on your GDPR project but they must be able to show that they have allocated enough time to remain fully aware of the progress of the project and understand the implications of the Regulation on the working practices of your company.

Decide your data types and who owns them

These will need to be represented on the project. List all the departments that hold or process personal data and where it comes from. You may have several departments or teams that use the same data, so these should be represented in the project.

Example:

A motor insurance company generates a customer record as a result of a telephone call from the applicant, or an internet record when they filled in a form on your website or as a result of a referral from an aggregator. Each of these routes may provide you with slightly different data fields and they may have different views on your retention policy and be aware of different suppliers who are given extracts of the data. The project manager will need to understand the implications of the various fields and business requirements on your retention policy and your rights to process the data.

Data Protection Impact Assessment (DPIA) is carried out in order to identify risks and issues and to determine appropriate mitigation. This will need to be addressed as part of your project. Under the 1998 DPA Act the ICO said that UK companies should conduct a PIA, and this process has been accepted by the rest of the EU as equivalent to the DPIA process.

Here is what the ICO says about the PIA process:

Key points:

- *A PIA is a process which assists organizations in identifying and minimizing the privacy risks of new projects or policies.*
- *Conducting a PIA involves working with people within the organization, with partner organizations and with the people affected to identify and reduce privacy risks.*
- *The PIA will help to ensure that potential problems are identified at an early stage, when addressing them will often be simpler and less costly.*
- *Conducting a PIA should benefit organizations by producing better policies and systems and improving the relationship between organizations and individuals.*

This will produce a gap analysis that you can address as part of the main project and from this you can see where you need to make decisions and what about. You can then ask "do you need all the fields that you are currently collecting?" For example, do you need to store a date of birth when a simple age indicator would suffice? If you are selling knives in the UK, you need to check that your customers are over 18, so ask them. If they are prepared to lie about that, they will probably also provide you with a false DOB, so storing the DOB may give you no additional benefit but a DOB will be more valuable to a hacker than simply knowing that a customer is "over 18". We will go into more detail in Section 8 – Data handling and management, below.

Create an action plan and from your project team(s)

This will have the time-scales and costs associated with the project and will need to be signed off by the Board. You will probably need a number of smaller, very specific and focused project teams to address the various issues that you have identified. If your organization uses a formal project management process, such as PRINCE 2, then this should be used for all of the smaller sub-projects so that the various project teams will be working to the same standards. If you don't use a formal project management process, then it may be worth considering employing a project manager to teach and control all of your project teams given the likely size of the GDPR project. We would not recommend running a GDPR project using "agile" techniques.

The role of IT

Your IT department will almost certainly have a significant role to play in the project. They will be the ones who will design and implement the facilities that you will need in order to comply with the decisions that the various business teams will request. In particular they will probably need to provide the departments with the facility for the deletion records when a customer has exercised their right to be forgotten. They will probably need to provide you with a facility to prevent processing if a customer has lodged an objection and the request is being evaluated. They may need to review your legacy systems to make sure they will provide you with the facilities that you will require and they will need to ensure that your decisions around your retentions policy can be implemented.

If you have old legacy systems that are still working but can no longer be updated, you need to look at these to make sure that you can meet the data portability rules and are able to delete selected records. Many early database systems will not let you delete records and if that is the case you will need to take alternative action before you have a valid request that you can't satisfy, for example, rendering data that you can't delete as inaccessible and/or un-readable.

Review what data your suppliers hold

Because data is at the very heart of the GDPR, it is vital that you know what data you hold and this will include data that you have passed on to a supplier.

You need to understand what you have sent them, both in terms of sensitivity and volume, how long they will retain it and how secure it is. You must also know if a supplier is processing data for you so that you can quickly identify who has it in the event of a request from a customer to amend incorrect data or to stop processing it. You will need to decide which of your suppliers will need to be subject to an audit to confirm that they are protecting your data correctly.

Review supplier contracts (with your legal and procurement departments), to determine which suppliers you will need to visit in order to conduct an audit to verify the answers that have been provided to you in response to your supplier questionnaire. You must ensure that if they are storing or processing personal data (for which you are responsible), then they must be compliant with the GDPR. You will need to keep track of the data they hold so that you know who to contact in the event of an instruction to stop processing the data belonging to an individual.

Definitions

- **Supplier:** As defined above, a supplier is any organization not part of your company or group of companies that provides a service to or handles data belonging to you.
- **Data:** For the purposes of this document, data is considered to be any information pertaining to customers, business or staff, and includes anonymized or generic information as well as specific identifiable information.
- **Service:** A service provided by a supplier may or may not involve the transfer, processing, storage or handling of your data. A service may also be the provision of goods, facilities, skills or knowledge. If the provision of a service is integral to the success or failure of your business then the service provider should be assessed to ensure that you have adequate controls in place.

Audit your suppliers

You should ensure that your key suppliers that store or process your data are able to protect it and that you know what data they hold. To do this you should arrange for them to be audited or complete a supplier questionnaire so that you have a record of their compliance with your standards. In Section 11 there is an example of a supplier questionnaire. By definition this is only an example of the sort of questions that you may wish to ask and it is supplied as a guide only. We have no knowledge of your business or the nature of the data that you hold but we hope that the questionnaire will be of help. Please feel free to modify it in any way that assists you to ensure that your Suppliers are protecting your data and your reputation.

Create a data privacy governance structure

Your current privacy practices will need to be reviewed, in particular your "security by design and default". We will go into this in detail in the section "Data".

This will provide the reporting lines and tell your staff who to tell in the event of a security breach.

Review your right to process

Look at your legal basis for processing your data. You must document your legal basis for processing and retain this so you can show the SA (the ICO in the case of the UK) in the event of an audit. You may be audited at any time, not just if you have a data breach.

We will look at your right to process in two ways: your right to process "normal data" and your right to process "special categories" of data.

Your right to process "normal" data will be one or more of six conditions as specified in Article 6, these are:

1. You have the clear and explicit consent of the data subject.
2. Processing is necessary for the performance of a contract with the data subject or to take steps to enter into a contract.
3. Processing is necessary in order for you to comply with a legal obligation.
4. Processing is necessary to protect the vital interests of the data subject or another person.
5. Processing is necessary for the performance of a task carried out in the public interest.
6. Processing is necessary for the purpose of legitimate interests pursued by the controller or a third party, except where such interests are overridden by the interests, rights or freedoms of the data subject.

There are ten lawful reasons for processing "Special Categories of Data" as explained in Article 9; these are:

1. Explicit consent of the data subject, unless reliance on consent is prohibited by EU or Member State law.
2. Processing is necessary for carrying out obligations under employment, social security or social protection law, or a collective agreement.
3. Processing is necessary to protect the vital interests of a data subject or another individual where the data subject is physically or legally incapable of giving consent.
4. Processing carried out by a not-for-profit body with a political, philosophical, religious or trade union aim provided the processing relates only to members

or former members (or those who have regular contact with it in connection with those purposes) and provided there is no disclosure to a third party without consent.

5. Processing relates to personal data manifestly made public by the data subject.
6. Processing is necessary for the establishment, exercise or defence of legal claims or where courts are acting in their judicial capacity.
7. Processing is necessary for reasons of substantial public interest on the basis of Union or Member State law which is proportionate to the aim pursued and which contains appropriate safeguards.
8. Processing is necessary for the purposes of preventative or occupational medicine, for assessing the working capacity of the employee, medical diagnosis, the provision of health or social care or treatment or management of health or social care systems and services on the basis of Union or Member State law or a contract with a health professional.
9. Processing is necessary for reasons of public interest in the area of public health, such as protecting against serious cross-border threats to health or ensuring high standards of healthcare and of medicinal products or medical devices.
10. Processing is necessary for archiving purposes in the public interest, or scientific and historical research purposes or statistical purposes in accordance with Article 89(1).

Many companies will look at gaining consent, thinking that this is the easiest way to have a legitimate reason for processing but that is true *only* if the data subject has genuine choice in the matter. We will go into more detail in the section on "data" below.

Check your incident response plan

Not all incidents will happen within normal working hours and if you are the victim of a targeted attack then it is more likely that this will happen outside of your normal business hours. An employee working extended or unsocial hours on an important project will need to know what to do in the event of a serious security incident.

Likewise, natural disasters are not confined to the normal business day and so you will need a plan and a dedicated team to put a plan into action if a disaster happens, say over the weekend, which may affect your ability to process information.

You should have an incident response plan that tells staff who to inform if there is an incident (not just a security breach as above). The incident team will be responsible for planning the recovery phase of the incident. Many incidents can be minimized if they are tackled quickly and effectively. This will happen best if staff know how to report an incident and to whom. If you have a Help or Service Desk, this can usually act as the focal point so that staff can call in to report a suspected incident. You should test your incident response plan with realistic scenarios so that the members of the team know what they are expected to do in a range of situations.

Your incident response plan will depend on a number of factors, not least will be the nature of your business. Many old companies that were operating "traditional" working hours are now trading on-line around the clock. It would be wise to review your incident plan to make sure that it is still fit for purpose.

Disaster Recovery and Business Continuity Plan

While you will need to update your incident response plan as part of your GDPR project this will be a good time to review your Disaster Recovery (DR) and Business Continuity Plan (BCP) to make sure that they have been updated where appropriate to ensure that there have not been any negative impacts on your operations. Be careful not to assume that a DR plan is the same as a BCP. A Disaster Recovery Plan is commonly used by an IT department to ensure that IT services are recovered in the event of a serious incident. A Business Continuity Plan is what the rest of the business will use whilst, for example, the IT department is recovering IT services. The two are not inter-changeable. For example, inclement weather that prevents your key personnel from getting to work would invoke your BCP, not DR.

Transitioning to BAU

General points

Many GDPR projects in organizations are still in a project state – surveys indicate as many as 50% in the UK. Typically, post 25 May 2018 project "tails" are on average 6 months, hence full transitioning to BAU has not occurred for many companies. This means there is a risk of project versus operational challenge. An obvious priority is to have clear accountability for what remains to be done throughout the transition and beyond.

You may have been compliant on 25 May 2018 but any subsequent change could undermine that. Hence, it's critical that GDPR is integrated into business and technology changes throughout the organization.

Compliance needs to be integrated into day-to-day activities:

- All departments will need to look at their working practices to ensure that they maintain GDPR compliance in the way that they handle data. There needs to be a clear oversight role too (in compliance/governance team?)
- Supplier monitoring and the addition of new suppliers must ensure that the suppliers are compliant and key suppliers are audited to ensure that they maintain compliance. Pay attention to any suppliers who are outside of the EU and any that re-locate. Engage with the procurement team throughout.
- Companies need to understand that the cost of getting it wrong may be far higher now than before, so look at security and compliance budgets.

Change management

Change management must incorporate GDPR by design throughout business change governance. This means notably:

- Mandating DPIAs early in the project framework or development lifecycle (catch them early) and any additional data flows will need to be checked for compliance.

GDPR requirements must be embedded into the design process e.g.:

- role-based access
- ability to extract data to meet data subject requests
- analysis of legal basis for personal data
- additional processing condition for special category data
- determination of retention period
- data minimization
- anonymization or deletion of data beyond retention period
- audit trail of consents, opt in/out.

Controller obligations in BAU

- clear roles and responsibilities for privacy, including DPO organization
- policies and procedures covering:

  ○ ongoing maintenance of processing inventory, privacy statements, consent forms
  ○ breach notification process

- vendor due-diligence and monitoring processes must cover information security and data protection
- vendor agreements must be in line with approved templates
- record-keeping requirements
- data transfers in line with approved policy/procedure.

Data subject rights in BAU

- Policies and procedures covering logging and tracking of data subject requests.
- Ensure that subject access requests are handled by well-tested processes within the one-month time-frame and have a mechanism to buy additional time if needed to reduce a peak as will happen if you suffer a data breach that becomes public knowledge.

Risk management and information security in BAU

- Extend existing risk management, policy, control and reporting framework to cover GDPR compliance risks e.g.:

  ◦ periodically obtaining assurance that policies are being adhered to and information security controls are operating effectively
  ◦ conducting audits on processors
  ◦ auditing and monitoring of controller and data subject Rights processes

- Data storage will need to be audited to ensure that only the required fields are stored to avoid mission creep and any redundant data fields identified and deleted.
- Data retention will also need to be subject to internal challenge.
- Testing breach notification and internal processes to report suspicious emails, phone-calls, unauthorized entry attempts etc. Thank staff who get it right.
- Understand cyber-attack trends and keep up to date with the methods that are used.
- Network monitoring may need to be enhanced to ensure that any potential breaches are identified quickly. Too many breaches are found to be months or even years old; this will be taken into account when looking at the level of a fine.

HR and communications in BAU

Staff awareness must be maintained and ways of engaging existing staff and particularly long service staff who may be comfortable that they know the systems. Keep it fresh and keep it personal.

- data protection is everyone's responsibility: this needs to be reflected in people's contracts and KPIs
- induction of new joiners
- ongoing training.

Section

6

Information security best practice

The need for a robust information security framework

The GDPR requires that Data Controllers *"shall implement appropriate technical and organizational measures to ensure and be able to demonstrate that processing is performed in accordance with this Regulation"* (Article 24(1)).

Article 5(2) also requires that the controller be responsible for and be able to demonstrate compliance with the guiding principles relating to processing of personal data.

These requirements can be met by implementing an information security framework. Such a framework will also introduce and provide a bedrock for good working practices that support Article 25 (Data protection by design and by default) and Article 32 (Security of processing).

Most businesses in the twenty-first century naturally implement *some* level of security simply by virtue that Microsoft have embedded security into their current operating systems. For example, a username and password, anti-virus software, software firewalls, automatic software updates. But it is one thing to have these essential services embedded by default and quite another to control access. But we will look at this and other cyber threats a little later.

Certainly, within Europe the implementation of formal risk-based information security frameworks has become the norm rather than the exception, the UK government even producing its own Security program to provide the most basic protection against cyber threats. The United States of America is starting to follow suit and the National Institute of Standards and Technology (NIST) has produced a framework for cyber security protection.

ISO27001/2:2013

The internationally recognized ISO27001 Information Security Management System (ISMS) was derived from the British Standard BS7799 (1995). It is dynamic in that only the framework controls that are applicable to your environment are used and flexible in that you choose how the controls are applied.

It is complex and it can take up to nine months to achieve certification working with an auditor from a UKAS-approved certification body (e.g. BSS).

There are fourteen compliance areas with each area comprising multiple recommendations. Part 1 will guide you through the requirements of the framework and Part 2 through its implementation. Irrespective of whether you opt to achieve certification or not, this is an excellent and internationally recognized framework and merely using the framework as a basis for information security will set your organization above others.

Either option, certification or compliance as a standard, is not for the faint-hearted and will require considerable commitment from the executive board and external assistance. You will need to fully understand risk and risk management, as the framework is an almost entirely risk-based approach to information security.

If your organization opts for the Certification route, your UKAS Auditor will guide you through the implementation stage and then carry out interim audits every six months to continually assess the implemented framework which is then followed up with a three-yearly re-certification audit.

Implementing an ISO27001 framework will require a budget in the region of £3K–£5K per annum for auditing and you will need the services of a full-time information security professional.

Implementing ISO27001

Implementing the ISO27001:2013 framework can be broken down into a number of steps. The framework centres around a document referred to as the Information Security Management System or ISMS. This is the document that describes how your organization is applying the security framework. Before you can draft this ISMS you have to undertake a risk assessment. This step is critical if you are to understand the threats and vulnerabilities that will ultimately enable you to calculate your risk. Next you must decide which of the ISO27001 controls you will need in order to mitigate your identified risk. This is called the "Statement of Applicability" or simply the "SOA". In this document you are stating which *controls* are *applicable* to your environment (both physical and technical). Once you are happy with your SOA you can start to implement the necessary measures to meet the controls and as these are implemented you can start to create your ISMS.

Whilst undoubtedly more expensive to implement and maintain than the cyber essentials framework, it is popular with organizations that collect and process large amounts of information as it demonstrates to their customers a commitment to good security and data management. Any organization that implements this framework will also stand out amongst peers when bidding for new business and for many it will obviate the need to complete tiresome security questionnaires. An anonymized Statement of Applicability and a facsimile of the ISO27001 Certificate will usually satisfy the most probing information security professional!

To find an ISO27001 Certification body visit https://www.ukas.com

The ISO2700 series of standards

It would be remiss of us not to mention the ISO27000 series. Currently (at the time of writing), there are some 44 discrete standards all of which are related to information security. They cover almost every scenario from the implementation of an ISMS (which we have covered) to guidelines for cyber security (ISO27032) to risk management (ISO27005), to cloud security (ISO27017) to incident investigation (ISO27043).

NIST security framework

The National Institute for Standards and Technology in the United States of America has introduced a framework for improving critical infrastructure cybersecurity. First published in 2014 the framework was revised in 2017 and is now available as an open-source framework as version 1.1 published in April 2018.

The framework provides a common language for understanding, managing, and expressing cybersecurity risk to internal and external stakeholders.

It can be used to help identify and prioritize actions for reducing cybersecurity risk and it is a tool for aligning policy, business, and technological approaches to managing that risk. It can be used to manage cybersecurity risk across entire organizations or it can be focused on the delivery of critical services within an organization.

NIST have mapped this framework to other common frameworks, for example: ISO27001:2013, COBIT 5, and CIS CSC. However, unlike the ISO27001 and UK Cyber Essentials program, there is no certification route. Nonetheless it is a detailed and effective security framework that may suit non-European organizations.

Further details on how to apply the NIST framework may be found here: https://nvlpubs.nist.gov/nistpubs/CSWP/NIST.CSWP.04162018.pdf

Cyber essentials

For companies operating in the United Kingdom who may be reluctant to make the leap into ISO27001, the UK government-backed Cyber Essentials cybersecurity certification scheme sets out a baseline for cybersecurity suitable for organizations in most sectors. The scheme addresses five key controls that, when implemented correctly, can prevent around 80% of cyber-attacks. The five key controls are:

1. secure configuration of networks
2. boundary firewalls and gateways
3. access control
4. patch management
5. malware protection.

Cyber Essentials is a very technical framework that most organizations will rely on their IT department or IT services supplier to implement. We'll take a very quick look at what each of the five controls mean:

Secure configuration. This relates to how your servers and workstations are configured for use, how they are accessed, supported, updated and protected.

Boundary firewalls and gateways. These provide protection from the Internet. Whilst anti-virus software will help protect against unwanted and harmful programs, a firewall helps in preventing would-be attackers from accessing your network in the first place and the gateway allows your users to access the internet safely.

Access controls. It is important that only those who *need* access to systems *have* that access. Most users will not need administrative access to servers, they just need access to documents that fall within their area of responsibility. As your employees move about the business, then their access requirements will change so this must also be controlled to avoid what is known as '**Privilege creep**' where users gain more and more access permissions.

Patch management. Patching is the activity of applying software updates to prevent low-level cyber-attack. Microsoft releases new updates every month, usually on the first Tuesday and this has come to be known as 'Patch Tuesday'. Whilst updates on user workstations are automatic, the requirements of servers have to be controlled, or managed – usually by your IT department or supplier.

Malware protection. Malicious software protection is not just virus protection but also Spyware, BotNet (Robotic Network) software and Ransomware – in fact any piece of code that is designed to corrupt, delete or steal your data. Firewalls won't protect your users from malicious software on websites but your Malware suites on your user workstations do.

There are two flavours of cyber essentials: **Cyber Essentials** and **Cyber Essentials Plus**. The former is through self-certification and will comprise the completion of a security questionnaire, an agreed scope of the network to be certified and finally an external vulnerability scan. You will need to contact an approved certification body and they will guide you through the five stages and run the scan when you are ready. Depending on the state of your security and network the entire process could be achieved in three to four weeks. The Cyber Essentials Plus program is more involved and will involve your certification company visiting your site and carrying out internal vulnerability scans and audit of your workstations and *modus operandi*.

You can find a certification company here: https://www.iasme.co.uk/certification-bodies/

The cost of obtaining a Cyber Essentials certificate will range from £300 to £1300 and from about £1400 to £2400 for Cyber Essentials Plus. Many certifying organizations will offer an on-line help service, so the more help you need, the more you pay.

Once you have obtained your Cyber Essentials or Cyber Essentials Plus certificate you will receive an official logo to place on your website but remember, it is recommended that you renew your certificate annually.

Security testing

Whichever method you choose to use to secure your infrastructure and applications you will need to test that your security is working. There are several ways to do this and they vary in cost and effectiveness. Which method you choose will depend on the value of your data and the risk that you calculate is posed to your organization and your customers.

Vulnerability scanning

Vulnerability scanning is an automated way of testing that your network infrastructure is patched and doesn't have any unnecessary ports or services open. Remember a vulnerability scan will not test your network defences, it will only advise you whether there are any aspects of your network which could be exploited by an attacker. While these tests are automated they are configurable and are as good basic check.

Penetration testing

The next level of testing is a penetration test, or pen test. These are more thorough than a vulnerability scan but many organizations like to undertake regular scans and then schedule an annual pen test. There are two forms of pen testing and these are:

Unauthenticated test

This is a test that uses no authentication, that is, a userid and password. The aim is to simulate how a would-be hacker might try and attack your network with no prior knowledge of your organisation or network other than what can be obtained via the Internet or other nefarious means, for example, identity theft or profiling. This form of attack may last from a few days to several weeks, depending upon the complexity of your infrastructure and how much you want to pay.

Authenticated test

As the name suggests, the authenticated test will make use of some form of authentication, particularly if you offer customers a sign-in account. The advantage of this type of test is that you will provide the consultant with a head-start and may even assist them to attack your systems so you may be confident that, if they are unable to gain access to your data without triggering an alarm, a hacker will also be unlikely to gain entry without spending a great deal of time and effort.

Tiger Attack

A "Tiger Attack" is commonly a predetermined physical and cyber-attack on your office and systems, particularly your network infrastructure. It is not *quite* the same as a penetration test as it could include email scams, "tailgating" into an office and all manner of underhand ways to test your security. There will need to be clear "'rules of engagement" for your Board to agree to. A Tiger Attack will often include phishing attacks to try to trick your staff into giving out vital information, as would be the case in a real hack.

Be sure to reward the staff who get their security right rather than blaming those who make a mistake. Make it clear that when a member of staff reports an attempt at social engineering, or a credible phishing attack, they are protecting the company and their jobs.

Risk

Information security is centred on risk. That is, the calculation of likelihood *times* impact. In order to apply an information security framework to your organization you must understand how to qualify and calculate risk.

Understanding risk

In information security terms, "risk" has to be a calculated number if it is to be of any use at all. The word "risk" is invariably used to describe an event that might happen. We may hear someone advise of a high risk of cyber-attack or a high risk of a terrorist attack. But what does that actually mean? That a cyber-attack is imminent? That it's bound to happen? The word "risk" is therefore often misused. In fact there is often the *likelihood* of a cyber-attack and there may from time to time be the *threat* of a terrorist attack but the *risk* is something quite different.

For example, a workstation without any anti-virus protection that is connected to the Internet is *vulnerable* to malicious software and therefore the *likelihood* or the *threat* of a cyber-criminal launching an attack is *high* and if this is successful the *impact* will be *high* – we may experience all of our data being corrupted. So, in fact, our *risk* is a consideration of all these factors – *threat, likelihood and impact*. We might also consider *capability* and *intent*. The attacker may have the *intent* to attack your network but doesn't have the *capability* or they may have the *capability* but have no *intent*.

Consider this scenario

Someone places their inexpensive, battered, cell phone on a table in a busy restaurant or bar. The phone (a physical asset) is not worth very much money and is only capable of retaining a few telephone numbers (information assets). Although it could easily be stolen its value is low, the thief couldn't re-sell the phone and if all that could be gained are a few telephone numbers then very little, if any, information would be of use. So we have a *low value* asset, and although it is *vulnerable* to theft the *likelihood* of such is *low* and even if it were stolen then the *impact* would be *low* since little data is stored and it has little value.

We therefore calculate the risk by multiplying *likelihood* x *impact* – taking into consideration factors such as *threat* and *vulnerability* hence we have the equation:

$$(\text{likelihood}) \text{ low} \times (\text{impact}) \text{ low} = (\text{risk}) \text{ low}$$

Now consider an alternative scenario

A state-of-the-art iPhone is placed on a table in the same busy restaurant or bar. The phone is worth a lot of money, it has a lot of information stored in its processor, for example: phone numbers, names, email addresses, software to gain remote access to an employer's network, banking details, and internet passwords. It is a valuable physical asset containing valuable information assets. Being left exposed on that table, it is highly *vulnerable* to the *threat* of theft. Before the evening is out it is highly *likely* that an attempt to steal the phone will be made and when this happens the loss of assets – physical and information – may have a potentially catastrophic *impact* on the owner, the business and all the people whose details are held in the phone's memory. Our risk calculation is now:

$$(\text{likelihood}) \text{ high} \times (\text{impact}) \text{ high} = (\text{risk}) \text{ high}$$

Assigning values

By assigning numerical values to our threat, likelihood and impact we can calculate risk value that has some meaning. A common table format for calculating risk is shown here:

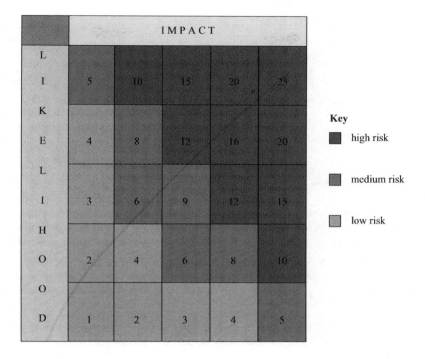

The key next to the table above shows the different areas that represent low, medium and high risks. To use this graph we evaluate the likelihood in the vertical column and the impact in the horizontal column and where the two values meet, this is the risk value.

So, if we take our inexpensive movable phone in scenario 1, we have estimated that the likelihood of theft is low (say 2) and the impact of the theft is also low (say 2 again) so our risk value is 4.

In scenario 2 we estimate the likelihood to be high – say 5 and the impact of theft high, say 5 so we have a risk value of 25.

By assigning a value, we would expect that after mitigation the risk value will be reduced even if the calculation remains in the 'high' band. For example, if likelihood of theft is reduced to medium by keeping the iPhone in a pocket, say 3, even though the impact value stays the same (i.e. it could still be stolen and data lost), the risk value calculation is now 15. We still have a high risk but *noticeably reduced*. Of course, in a real-life situation the iPhone will be fully encrypted and password protected so the risk is reduced further, the only impact being the loss of a physical asset.

The resulting risk calculation after mitigation is called the *residual risk* and the value of risk we may be prepared to accept without any further mitigation is called the *risk appetite*. On our table any risk value below 9 is considered to be within appetite. If we were dealing with highly valuable assets we might decide to lower our risk appetite.

Mitigation	Remediation action
Reduce	Apply controls to reduce vulnerability or likelihood in order to reduce overall risk calculation
Accept	If it is not viable to reduce vulnerability or likelihood then the risk must be accepted. Sometime this may be the only course if further action impedes a business goal
Transfer	Transfer the risk to an entity better able to manage it. For example, placing all your personal data in a secure off-site data centre managed by a third party.
Avoid	Probably the most difficult mitigation and could involve the termination of a project entirely.

Risk mitigation

In true Risk Management terms, *risk mitigation* is the act of applying remediation actions to either **reduce, accept, transfer** or **avoid** risk.

Undertaking a risk analysis

This activity is mandatory if the organization is seeking compliance and/or certification to the ISO27001 framework and is absolutely necessary for completing a DPIA (or DPA) for GDPR compliance. For most, a simple spreadsheet will suffice to record the details. It is important to record *why* and *when* the risk analysis is being carried out as the completed document will provide evidence to an auditor and also a reminder to the business over time of the identified risks that have either been accepted or need monitoring. Your spreadsheet should not be over-complicated and must contain only relevant facts and not assumptions.

Risk Treatment Registers

The management of risk is an important activity for information security and GDPR compliance and when properly managed will provide the business with valuable information, not least if it is ever unfortunate enough to suffer a data breach. The Risk Treatment Register (or simply RTR) contains all known risks that have been identified from the risk analysis and, as the name suggests, is a record of what mitigation against risk has been undertaken, when and why. It should look very similar to the risk analysis spreadsheet but will typically contain less detail.

Risk analysis as part of your DPIA

When you undertake your DPIA you are looking at your intended processing of personal and/or sensitive data so you must identify whether any of your processing activities will have an impact (and hence risk) to that data. Risk analysis of data holdings is carried out in the same manner as for any other aspect of security. You are recording the types of data you hold and it is the author's opinion that you should record all data holdings, not just personal and sensitive data in an *Information Asset Register*. When this is complete each type of data can be assessed to identify whether there is any risk, that is:

- Is the data vulnerable?
- What is the likelihood of any vulnerability being exploited?
- What would be the impact of any exploitation?

Once we have these parameters identified we can calculate our risk score and then apply appropriate mitigation to reduce that risk.

Assessing your suppliers for security

As a data controller you have the responsibility for ensuring that data processing activities comply with the Regulation (Article 24) and this may mean that you have to establish that any third-party supplier is also complying with the Regulation (Article 28).

Data is a vital part of your business and safe keeping of that data is of utmost importance in order to protect financial interests, maintain regulatory compliance, and to protect company brand and reputation.

Prior to releasing any data to an organization outside of your company or group, the supplier should undergo a review of their IT security which will typically include an analysis of their technical security, operational platforms, procedures and processes, documentation, or any other aspect deemed appropriate dependent upon the service to be provided.

Increasingly it is becoming common practice to ask your current or potential supplier to complete a questionnaire on their security processes. This should not be over-complicated or your supplier may simply refuse to answer questions. Indeed, a supplier who has achieved a certified level of security may just provide you with a statement. This is okay as long as they also provide you with a copy of their certificate and at least a statement from their Board of Directors.

However, you should be prepared to provide your supplier with a questionnaire and we include a typical example in Section 11, Assessing your suppliers.

Key areas of security you should consider

Although aimed at your supplier, you might also consider asking such questions of you own business.

Organization

You should establish whether data is stored in countries and with companies where appropriate regulations and guidelines are applicable.

Data stored with a cloud service provider, where geographic location of the data cannot be clearly stated, should consider the reputation and size of the service provider.

- data to be stored within the UK is preferred
- data to be stored within the EU is generally acceptable to any regulators.

Data to be stored within a non-EU country that adheres to the GDPR and is on the EU list of countries that it accepts as compliant is acceptable.

- Data to be stored in any other country should be considered as a possible risk and it will be up to you to ensure that the supplier complies with the GDPR. You can do this by having a carefully worded contract that ensures that the organization will comply with the Regulation.

Payment Card Industry/Data Security Standard (PCI/DSS)

You should know if you are required to comply with the requirements of the Payment Card Industry Data Security Standards. If you don't handle any payment details at all then you can ignore the PCI/DSS requirements. If you use a payment provider, such as PayPal or WorldPay, then you need to ensure that your IT systems are PCI compliant. If in doubt, you should speak with your merchant provider to be sure.

Security policy

Do you have a documented information security policy and management systems in line with external industry recognized standards such as ISO27000? Are these:

- communicated to, understood and accepted by all employees, suppliers, and agents, at time of enrolment and at regular intervals ongoing
- regularly reviewed to be kept relevant with emerging technology and threats
- supported by senior management
- inclusive of incident and change management procedures.

You should indicate accountability and segregation of duties for information security and you should also indicate that, where a sub-contractor is used in the provision of the service, or where a sub-contractor is permitted access to your data, that comparative policies are maintained.

Your supplier should indicate that

- access to your data is provided on a need-only basis
- access permission allocations and revocations are auditable
- service activity and data access is auditable.

Network access controls

You should indicate that appropriate network segregation exists and that:

*   development, testing and production environments are distinct
*   networks and systems used to provide the service are segregated from other functions
*   intrusion attempts and malicious activity generate system reactions
*   access from an external connection is restricted and auditable
*   use of wireless networking is restricted and auditable

Server and PC protection, physical and environmental security

You should indicate that procedures are defined for

*   patch management and anti-virus updates
*   secure disposal of computer equipment, digital storage media, and printed material.

You should indicate that networks and systems are protected against:

*   fire
*   flood
*   power interruptions
*   unauthorized physical access.

You should indicate that secure backup procedures are defined and that data in storage or transit is appropriately encrypted and secured.

European Data Protection Board (EDPB)

The EDPB is an EU body responsible for the application of the GDPR. It is charged with ensuring that it remains consistent and up-to-date across all member countries.

For its latest workings see **https://edpb.europa.eu/**

Section

7

Awareness

Information security policy

The starting point for any awareness campaign may well be your existing information security policy or a codes of practice document. Here is an example of what might be in your document.

1. Statement from your Chairman, CEO, MD or other senior Director

   a) This will demonstrate the commitment of the Board to the principle of information security.

2. Information security principles

   a) Information security is the responsibility of your organization and cannot be delegated to any third party (a particular enhancement within GDPR).
   b) Key Risk Indicators (KRI) and Key Performance Indicators (KPI), techniques and procedures will be maintained to measure the effectiveness of information security.
   c) The value of each major information asset will be determined by risk assessment
   d) Protection of each asset will be appropriate to the value of the asset and the threat that it faces.
   e) Each asset will have an owner who will be responsible for its protection.
   f) Only authorized and licensed software will be used within your organization.
   g) All users of your organization's information assets will receive appropriate training to ensure they are able to fulfil their individual responsibilities towards information security.

h) Users of your organization's information assets must be aware of their value and safeguard them accordingly.

i) Information security concerns and breaches must be reported in accordance with escalation procedures.

j) Managers have prime responsibility for security in the areas they manage.

k) Users of your organization's information and systems will be responsible for the security of information under their control.

l) Failure to comply with the Information Security Policy may result in disciplinary proceedings.

m) We will comply with all relevant regulatory, legal and licence obligations.

3. Organization

a) This section will detail the various management levels and responsibilities for the security of the company information assets. This would be a good place to insert a structure chart.

b) The role of the Data Protection Officer and Information Security Manager should be made clear so that your staff know that they are operating with the backing of the Board.

c) The responsibilities of information owners, users and custodians should be made clear.

d) A standard approach such as a RACI method could be adopted to clarify accountability.

4. Information classification

a) How you classify your data will depend on the nature of your business and the type of data that you hold.

b) Special classes of data, such as payment data covered by the PCI rules or sensitive personal data or data relating to HR or health information and also any information relating to children which requires special care.

5. Personnel security (*Ensuring your employees are aware of security*)

a) phishing scams
b) spear phishing
c) tailgating
d) bogus helpdesk calls

6. Physical and environmental security

a) Data centre locations and who may enter, who may authorize entry.

b) Environmental considerations (the need for IT equipment to be in an air-conditioned environment).

c) Fault reporting of IT equipment.

d) Special care when disposing of IT equipment (particularly recording material such as hard-drives, CDs or DVDs with data on them).
e) What external media, if any, may be connected to the company network or computers.
f) What process to follow if data needs to be moved between one data centre and another.
g) Clear-desk policy.

7. Computer and network management.

a) the need for system documentation.
b) segregation of duties (to avoid a single point of failure)
c) where development and operational areas will exist and how to move apps and data between them (see also 8.c)
d) special care when using 3rd party companies or contractors
e) capacity planning to avoid outgrowing your system capacity.
f) anti-virus precautions
g) who to report a suspected virus to
h) who to report a suspected security breach to (this will become very important under the GDPR)
i) software considerations to avoid the use of unlicensed software
j) data loss prevention rules
k) auditing of resources and staff
l) operating system and application patching rules
m) data backups
n) fault reporting
o) wireless router rules (including guest network segment and how this will be segregated from the production network)
p) encryption standards and what algorithms may be used, and what key management rules there are
q) media handling rules (such as file attachments, links in emails, connecting to unknown websites etc.)

8. System access control

a) What rules apply to the use of personal devices— Bring Your Own Device (BYOD).
b) Who can authorize a request to access data?
c) Change control procedure for introducing new applications or updating existing ones.
d) Access is to be given on a "need to" basis.
e) Users should have the least privilege in order to do their job (they should not be given the authority to change or delete data if they only need to read it).
f) System access will be recorded and audited.

9. System development and maintenance
10. Business continuity planning
11. Compliance

    a) a statement that the company will comply with your National Data Protection Laws (and GDPR), Payment Card Industry Standards, any regulatory bodies that your company are controlled by, or report to
    b) special care with using social media when connecting from a company account
    c) any "official comments" must be authorized by management
    d) data retention policy
    e) external audits
    f) penetration testing of the network security.

12. Acceptable use policy.

    a) what staff may and may not do "in the name of the company"
    b) what sites staff may use from company devices or networks
    c) what standards of language and respect are expected of staff when dealing with one another or with customers.

Induction

Having a formal induction process for all employees is essential to ensuring that information security and data protection is going to be at the heart of your business processes.

At the Induction your HR department should provide all attendees with copies of key policies and the location of these on your corporate network. All employees should be asked to confirm that they have read and understood security and data protection polices at least annually. This protects both the employee and the business in the event of a legal challenge.

Refresh and update

Policies should be reviewed and updated appropriately at least annually or whenever there is a change to the business operation or when new legislation is introduced. This action will count towards the GDPR requirement of Data Protection by Default and Design.

Your policies should be concise and presented in such a way as to make them understandable and for employees to be able to find the information they need quickly. It will also make it easier for the designated management committee to update them!

Awareness

Information security is all about bringing cyber-threats into daily life, not by scaring your work-force but by informing them of what the threats are, how to recognize those threats and how to report them. Never berate an employee for missing a threat, instead use such an incident to inform and train others. If an employee highlights a threat which is subsequently avoided, then applaud them and again use the incident to inform others. Information security is not just for the workplace; your employees must embed good working practices into their daily lives so that security, again, becomes a default action by all.

World or local disasters can often lead to cyber-crime and employees may be the victims of scam emails for example requesting financial assistance. Your security manager should be ready to offer advice to employees. Public holidays and major festivals are also a time when cyber-crime is rife so again, this is the period when your awareness program should be ramped up

Security testing

Security testing is used to check the ability of your systems and staff to withstand an attack on your applications and infrastructure. There are a number of forms of security testing and these are covered in Section 6, Information security best practice.

A "Tiger Attack" is commonly a predetermined physical and cyber-attack on your office and systems, particularly your network infrastructure. It is not *quite* the same as a "Penetration test" as it could include email scams, "tailgating" into an office and all manner of underhand ways to test your security. There will need to be clear "rules of engagement" for your Board to agree to.

Be sure to reward the staff who get their security right rather than blaming those who make a mistake. Make it clear that when a member of staff reports an attempt at social engineering, or a credible phishing attack, they are protecting the company and their jobs.

Incident response plan

In Section 9 we look at the basic structure of an incident response plan. An important element in having a workable plan is to ensure that your staff are aware of the plan and what is expected of them. They need to understand what they should do if they suspect that an incident is happening or has occurred and who they should report it to.

It is important that all your staff understand the reporting process for normal working times and for out of hours. If they receive a suspicious email on a work's device out of hours, this should be reported and not left until the next working day for example. Early reporting will often help to reduce the impact of a security breach and may enable you to disrupt it before too much damage has been done.

Whistle-blowing policy/Hot-line

See if you can set up a whistle-blowing hot-line. If your organization is not large enough to justify the expense of your own hot-line, see if you can team up with other small companies to share one.

Section
8

Data handling and management

Data holdings and retention

List the various sources of data that you hold and from this you can start to see if you need the data. For example, you may need to know if your customers are over 18 and for this people may have been asked for their date of birth. If you simply need to know that someone is over or under a given age, then ask them. It is less sensitive to ask for a particular age than it is to store your customer's date of birth.

The GDPR will be a good time to review what you are holding. If you can reduce the volume of data or rationalize the various data fields that you hold, you may be able to reduce the value of your data to a criminal. This will reduce your chance of being the victim of a hacker, or a group of hackers.

Understand the value of your data

Data is a valuable asset and should your data become corrupted, deleted, lost or fall into the hands of unauthorized persons either by accident or by theft then the consequences will be very serious indeed. The criminal fraternity will go to great lengths to obtain data which can then be used to discredit a business or, more likely, to be sold to the highest bidder. Whilst your data is valuable to you in order to run your business, to the criminal it possibly has a far greater monetary value.

This presents you with a challenge in terms of protecting your data so the more you can do make your data less vulnerable to the threat of theft the better. You should bear in mind that theft of data may not necessarily come from outside the business; the "internal threat" from employees, contractors and consultants can be significant, either through malicious intent or accident. This does not necessarily mean you need to harden your technical security but limiting the number of fields and the amount of time you hold the data as much as possible renders the data less valuable to the attacker yet still remaining valuable to your business.

Data ownership

List your data files by ownership. All of the departments that own personal data will need to be involved in the project. Break down ownership by department, e.g.:

1. HR
2. Sales
3. Marketing
4. Research
5. Accounts

    a) at normal times
    b) during the close period – if this applies to your company

6. Board papers

You need to record who owns what data so that in the event of an incident you can easily see who to contact. It is important that all data-sets have an owner. Typically, ownership will follow the hierarchical management structure of the organization – so the head of Finance would be the owner of all finance data, the head of HR will own all HR data and so on.

Within this we can define the data types as:

Public – this is data that you publish and might include:

a) your policies,
b) product descriptions,
c) non-sensitive financial data
d) product advertising.

Data that you publish should not be able to identify a natural living person and should therefore be outside of the scope of the GDPR.

Company confidential – This will be data such as:

a) accounts
b) formulae
c) corporate contracts
d) take-over plans
e) growth plans etc.

While this data may be very valuable to your organization and not for public consumption, it should probably not be personal data and therefore not subject to the GDPR.

Company data, such as

a) HR
b) direct customer data (that you obtained from the data subjects)
c) bought in data (not from the data subjects)
d) shareholder data
e) accounts data where the data can identify a living individual who traded with your company.

This *is* personal data and all of these data types must be included in the GDPR project:

Sensitive data, referred to as **"special categories"** will be data that contains any of the following:

a) racial or ethnic origin
b) political opinions
c) religious or philosophical beliefs
d) trade union membership
e) genetic or biometric data for the purpose of uniquely identifying the individual
f) health
g) data concerning a person's sex life or sexual orientation.

Processing the above categories of personal data is prohibited unless you can fulfil one of a number of special categories, which we will go into later in the section "Lawfulness of processing special categories of data".

Secret data which **may** be exempt from the GDPR:

a) military secret
b) criminal or terrorist information
c) data relating to a current criminal investigation.

If you are working for the government, police or an organization that is working under the direction of the government, then you may be exempted from the GDPR by the nature of the sensitivity of the information you are processing for that data but you will probably also hold data that is covered by the Regulation. For these data types you must ensure that you know which data types are exempt from the Regulation and which are still covered.

Data Protection Impact Assessment – DPIA

A DPIA is not needed for all projects but if you conduct a DPIA as part of your regular project process, you will be able to see what risks you are taking and how you will mitigate them. It will also demonstrate your commitment to risk identification and reduction in your normal work.

A DPIA is mandatory if you are processing or storing data that may result in a high risk to the data subject. The definition of "high risk" is not spelt out in the GDPR and therefore you may view your data as not being high risk in your own risk analysis but your nominated SA may take a different view, particularly if you suffer a serious security breach. You need to work out the risk and while this may seem like Catch 22, you may conclude that a DPIA is a worthwhile exercise anyway as it will help you identify redundant data.

The DPIA process should describe the data flows into and out of your organization. It should then identify the privacy risks and identify the solutions to the risks or define who is responsible for accepting the risks.

The following extract (in italics) is taken from the Information Commissioner's Office [Conducting privacy impact assessments code of practice – 25/02/2014 Version 1.0], licensed under the Open Government Licence.

What do we mean by privacy?

Privacy, in its broadest sense, is about the right of an individual to be let alone. It can take two main forms, and these can be subject to different types of intrusion:

- *Physical privacy – the ability of a person to maintain their own physical space or solitude. Intrusion can come in the form of unwelcome searches of a person's home or personal possessions, bodily searches or other interference, acts of surveillance and the taking of biometric information*
- *Informational privacy – the ability of a person to control, edit, manage and delete information about themselves and to decide how and to what extent such information is communicated to others. Intrusion can come in the form of collection of excessive personal information, disclosure of personal information without consent and misuse of such information. It can include the collection of information through the surveillance or monitoring of how people act in public or private spaces and through the monitoring of communications whether by post, phone or online and extends to monitoring the records of senders and recipients as well as the content of messages*

Privacy risk is the risk of harm arising through an intrusion into privacy. This code is concerned primarily with minimizing the risk of informational privacy – the risk of harm through use or misuse of personal information. Some of the ways this risk can arise are through personal information being:

- *inaccurate, insufficient or out of date;*
- *excessive or irrelevant;*
- *kept for too long;*
- *disclosed to those who the person it is about does not want to have it;*
- *used in ways that are unacceptable to or unexpected by the person it is about; or*
- *not kept securely.*

Harm can present itself in different ways. Sometimes it will be tangible and quantifiable, for example financial loss or losing a job. At other times it will be less defined, for example damage to personal relationships and social standing arising from disclosure of confidential or sensitive information. Sometimes harm might still be real even if it is not obvious, for example the fear of identity theft that comes from knowing that the security of information could be compromised. There is also harm which goes beyond the immediate impact on individuals. The harm arising from use of personal information may be imperceptible or inconsequential to individuals, but cumulative and substantial in its impact on society. It might for example contribute to a loss of personal autonomy or dignity or exacerbate fears of excessive surveillance. The outcome of a PIA should be a minimization of privacy risk. An organization will need to develop an understanding of how it will approach the broad topics of privacy and privacy risks. There is not a single set of features which will be relevant to all organizations and all types of project – a central government department planning a national crime prevention strategy will have a different set of issues to consider to an app developer programming a game which collects some information about users. Understanding privacy risk in this context does though require an understanding of the relationship between an individual and an organization. Factors that can have a bearing on this include:

- *reasonable expectations of how the activity of individuals will be monitored*
- *reasonable expectations of the level of interaction between an individual and an organization*
- *the level of understanding of how and why particular decisions are made about people.*

This means that you should look at your data holding from a business point of view and also as a customer would view it. While it may seem worthwhile to have all the information you have ever been told about a customer, this will also increase the value to a criminal and the impact of a security breach.

Data protection by design and default

The GDPR is very focused on making systems and applications secure and organizations security conscious. Article 25 relates to "Data protection by design and by default."

It is always easier and cheaper to build security into a project or application than to retrofit it but many organizations see security as an "added extra" that will delay the project. The fact is that by including security as part of your core design you will often identify potential problems at an early stage and be able to design around them with little impact on the time-scales or budget. Have data protection as part of your BAU process and ensure that it is considered at the start of every project.

We looked at risk assessment and security in Section 6 – Information security best practice as well as looking at the security of your data content in this Section under "Defensive Data".

The data flows

Data flows will be of four main types:

- data that you obtain from other organizations
- data that you obtain directly from the data subject
- data that you send back to your customers
- data that you send to other organizations (and also information that these organizations then pass on to other organizations).

In order to know what data you obtain from other organizations you also need to know what data you need to obtain from them and what data you do obtain from them. You should also use the DPIA as an opportunity to review your data retention policy, so you only keep data for as long as you need to.

Example

We will look at the case of an insurance company sending a customer record to a garage in order to have the customer's car repaired following an accident. The information that the garage will need will be different from the information that a medical practitioner will need, even though both sets of information will come from the insurance company claims system. The garage will need to know the name, address, contact telephone number(s) and vehicle description as well as details of the damage that the garage is being asked to repair. They will not be expected to repair any pre-existing damage to the vehicle, so the details of the damage are important but the garage does not need to know about any injuries to the occupants of the vehicle. They will not need to know about any passengers, or damage sustained to any other vehicle, so they will only need to receive and store some information relating to the accident.

Reflections

From the above example it is clear that part of the DPIA is to ensure that the system is only recording the data fields that they need. If they have been sent more data than they need, the organization should not be recording the excess fields.

For each of your systems you should list the data fields that you receive, what you process and store and what data you send on to a supplier.

Data coming in

List the data fields that you obtain and where this comes from. Some data may not be personal under the existing data protection law but will become personal under the GDPR, so if you are collecting the IP address of the customer's computer or router, this was not considered personal data under the earlier Data Protection Acts but is under the current DPA and the GDPR. If you need this information, particularly if you use this to help identify the customer and detect a possible invalid log-on in future, then you should continue to collect this but you must note this as part of your DPIA or PIA – see "Your GDPR project" earlier.

You should review who, within your organization, has access to this data. This is of great importance to a company that is growing. Your working practices may have been proportionate and sensible when you had a handful of employees but as your organization grows and departments become more specialized then you should look again at the data that they have access to and decide if it is still appropriate.

Some of the data may be obtained directly from your customers and some may come from other organizations. Use this as an opportunity to review the data that you collect and store. You are only allowed to use data that you have a "need" to, so confirm that you need all the data fields that you are collecting and storing and remove any that you no longer require.

Data going out

Where you send data is very important. If you send data to the customer as part of your business process, you should review what you are sending them and how. If they see their data when they connect to your website and do this on an encrypted line (HPPTS), then you should have a good degree of confidence in the security of the data but if you send them an email, you will need to be very careful what data you include.

If you send customer data to a supplier, then you must ensure that you do this as securely as possible and confirm that the supplier needs all of the data that you send them; make sure they are processing and storing it securely, see Chapter 11, Assessing your suppliers.

Risk assessment

A key element of the DPIA is to assess the risks that you face in the way that you collect, process, store and send on data. While risk management should be part of your normal project management process, many companies see risks as simply risks to the delivery or cost of the project and while these are important risks to manage, the risk to the customer and your company from data corruption or loss must be taken into account. All risks should be assessed and mitigated where necessary.

Some risks will need to be treated with additional caution, so if you are storing data for young children, where you know the child's age, then you must use extra caution.

You need to assess the risk to the individual, the risk to your company and compliance risks and record these.

Refer to Section 6 for more information on risk analysis and management.

Risks to the individual

These are where you have inadequate controls over who you disclose data to.

Merging data, as in a "Big Data Project", may mean that the context of the data has changed or that the amount of data you hold has increased and you are now holding data that you have no justified business need to hold.

If you use anonymized data, then make sure that you have not revealed too much detail that would allow the individual to be identified especially by using a number of "real" fields. You may keep a town name and details of the makeup of the family, along with details of the house, or their cars. It may be possible for a data analyst or a criminal to identify the precise address from several fields, that alone would not be seen as intrusive.

A Ransomware attack, where a criminal will infect your network with an auto-encrypting virus and then demand a payment before they will provide the decryption key is becoming more and more common. If your network experiences this type of attack then all the while you are investigating and hopefully halting the attack, a good deal of your data may have become encrypted and is therefore unavailable. By having good and regular backups, you may be able to restore your data without having to pay the criminals. The risk of having too many backups is that you may be keeping copies of data that you have been instructed to delete or modify.

Anonymization and pseudonymization

Earlier versions of the DPA spoke of anonymizing or pseudonymizing data, but it was not mandated that either of these techniques would be done at that time. In Article 25 the GDPR states:

1.   *Taking into account the state of the art, the cost of implementation and the nature, scope, context and purposes of processing as well as the risks of varying likelihood and*

severity for rights and freedoms of natural persons posed by the processing, the controller shall, both at the time of the determination of the means for processing and at the time of the processing itself, implement appropriate technical and organizational measures, such as pseudonymization, which are designed to implement data-protection principles, such as data minimization, in an effective manner and to integrate the necessary safeguards into the processing in order to meet the requirements of this Regulation and protect the rights of data subjects.

2. *The controller shall implement appropriate technical and organizational measures for ensuring that, by default, only personal data which are necessary for each specific purpose of the processing are processed. That obligation applies to the amount of personal data collected, the extent of their processing, the period of their storage and their accessibility. In particular, such measures shall ensure that by default personal data are not made accessible without the individual's intervention to an indefinite number of natural persons.*

The GDPR defines pseudonymized data thus:

'pseudonymization' means the processing of personal data in such a manner that the personal data can no longer be attributed to a specific data subject without the use of additional information, provided that such additional information is kept separately and is subject to technical and organizational measures to ensure that the personal data are not attributed to an identified or identifiable natural person (GDPR Article 4 (5))

Recital 26 states:

Whereas the principles of protection must apply to any information concerning an identified or identifiable person; whereas, to determine whether a person is identifiable, account should be taken of all the means likely reasonably to be used either by the controller or by any other person to identify the said person; whereas the principles of protection shall not apply to data rendered anonymous in such a way that the data subject is no longer identifiable; whereas codes of conduct within the meaning of Article 27 may be a useful instrument for providing guidance as to the ways in which data may be rendered anonymous and retained in a form in which identification of the data subject is no longer possible.

Anonymization and pseudonymisation are different, either can be used to protect your customers, your data and the reputation of your organization. What method you use, if any, will depend on the value of the data and the risk to the individuals that your data storage represents. If you are storing a customer's name, address, data of birth, bank account details and their mother's maiden name for example, you will need to take great care and ensure that you protect the records. Similarly, if you are storing a large volume of data, then the chance of your being a target of a hacker grows as the volume of data also grows.

Earlier data protection laws recognized the case for anonymizing data to protect the identity of the data subjects. In 2012 the ICO issued a paper *Anonymisation: managing data protection risk code of practice* and this is still valid today and is worth a read. We provide some extracts to give a flavour of the extent of the advice given. The paper stated:

The DPA does not require Anonymisation to be completely risk free – you must be able to mitigate the risk of identification until it is remote. If the risk of identification is reasonably likely the information should be regarded as personal data – these tests have been confirmed in binding case law from the High Court. Clearly, 100% Anonymisation is the most desirable position, and in some cases, this is possible, but it is not the test the DPA requires.

We use the term 're-identification' to describe the process of turning anonymised data back into personal data through the use of data matching or similar techniques. The code's annexes contain examples of various Anonymisation and re-identification techniques and illustrations of how anonymized data can be used for various purposes.

We use the broad term 'Anonymisation' to cover various techniques that can be used to convert personal data into anonymized data. We draw a distinction between Anonymisation techniques used to produce aggregated information, for example, and those – such as pseudonymization – that produce anonymized data but on an individual-level basis. The latter can present a greater privacy risk, but not necessarily an insurmountable one. We also draw a distinction between publication to the world at large and the disclosure on a more limited basis – for example to a particular research establishment with conditions attached.

In annex 3 of the paper there are some examples of different types of Anonymization techniques but it is stressed that the ICO is not advocating any particular method, and it will be the responsibility of the company to assess the best solution for their particular situation.

Within the GDPR the term "Pseudonymized data" is defined in several places. Recital 26 states:

The principles of data protection should apply to any information concerning an identified or identifiable natural person. Personal data which have undergone pseudonymization, which could be attributed to a natural person by the use of additional information should be considered to be information on an identifiable natural person. To determine whether a natural person is identifiable, account should be taken of all the means reasonably likely to be used, such as singling out, either by the controller or by another person to identify the natural person directly or indirectly. To ascertain whether means are reasonably likely to be used to identify the natural person, account should be taken of all objective factors, such as the costs of and the amount of time required for identification, taking into consideration the available technology at the time of the processing and technological developments. The principles of data protection should therefore not apply to anonymous information, namely information which does not relate to an identified or identifiable natural person or to personal data rendered anonymous in such a manner that the data subject is not or no longer identifiable. This Regulation does not therefore concern the processing of such anonymous information, including for statistical or research purposes.

Recital 29 states:

In order to create incentives to apply pseudonymization when processing personal data, measures of pseudonymization should, whilst allowing general analysis, be possible within the same controller when that controller has taken technical and organizational measures necessary to ensure, for the processing concerned, that this Regulation is implemented, and that additional information for attributing the personal data to a specific data subject is kept separately. The controller processing the personal data should indicate the authorized persons within the same controller.

Data retention

For every type of data that you store or process you need to record how long you will retain it. Generally, you may need to allow for "live" data and "used" data. Take the case of a merchant who sells items to customers and the customers have an account. For these cases, the data will be retained for as long as the customer continues to use their account, but should you retain the complete buying history? You may decide that this is justified as it allows you to see how loyal the customer is and therefore allows you to exercise discretion when dealing with a complaint.

So, how do you identify a customer who has stopped being a customer? If you know that they are no longer trading with you, it is a fairly simple decision to make, you will just have to decide how much history you keep and for how long. But if the customer simply stops buying, do you continue to store their data for months or years? What if they return and you then treat them as a new customer? That could give a very bad impression.

The fact is that every department or data owner will need to consider their retention policy in relation to their business model and record it. Your IT Team will probably need to implement the means for the system to purge redundant data. So long as you can justify in reasonable terms your decision and so long as you allow a customer to choose to have their records deleted, you should be OK. As with many aspects of the GDPR, you must record your decision and be able to justify it.

Binding corporate rules

If you transfer data between different parts of an organization or to a company that is outside of the EU, you will need to have "binding corporate rules" in place. This is a contract that states that the non-EU entity will be bound by the GDPR as far as your data is concerned.

The rules will need to be enforced and need to include:

1. The company has a duty to accept the BCR and be bound by them.
2. The creation of third-party rights for data subjects including the possibility to lodge a complaint before a competent Data Protection Authority (the ICO in the UK) and the courts.

3. The company accepts liability for paying compensation and to remedy breaches of the BCR.
4. The company has sufficient assets.
5. The burden of proof will be with the company and not with an individual making a complaint. The company will need to accept that they will need to prove that it was not responsible for a suspected breach.
6. There is easy access to the BCR for data subjects and easy access to information about the third-party beneficiary rights.
7. There must be evidence of a suitable training program for the staff of the third-party.
8. There must be a complaint handling process.
9. There must be an audit program covering the BCR.
10. There must be a network of privacy officers to oversee the handling of complaints and clear oversight with the BCR.
11. A duty to cooperate with the Data Protection Authorities.
12. A description of the data transfers covered by the BCR.
13. A statement of the geographical and material scope of the BCR (nature of the data, type of data subjects and the countries).
14. A process for updating the BCR.
15. A description of the privacy principles including the rules on transfers or onward transfers out of the EU.
16. The list of entities bound by the BCR.
17. A need to be transparent where national legislation prevents the group from complying with the BCR.
18. A statement about the relationship between national laws and the BCR.

Lawful processing

The legal basis for collecting and storing the personal data needs to be established and documented. As specified in Article 6, you must be aware that:

1. you have the permission of the data subject
2. processing is necessary for the performance of a contract with the data subject
3. processing is necessary for compliance with a legal obligation
4. processing is necessary for protecting the vital interests of the data subject or another person
5. processing is necessary for the performance of a task carried out in the public interest or in the exercise of official authority vested in the controller
6. processing is necessary for the purpose of legitimate interests pursued by the controller or a third party, except where such interests are overridden by the interests, rights or freedoms of the data subject.

Many companies will look at gaining consent, thinking that this is the easiest way to have a legitimate reason for processing but that is true only if the Data Subject a has genuine choice in the matter.

The Information Commissioner has issued guidance in the form of a number of documents. There are two that are very helpful when looking at the subjects of lawfulness of processing and consent, these are "Guide to the General Data Protection regulation (GDPR)" and "Consultation: GDPR consent guidance"; these are very helpful and worth a read. On the subject of consent, she said that: "For processing to be lawful under the GDPR, you need to identify (and document) your lawful basis for the processing. There are six lawful bases listed in Article 6(1), and consent is one of them.

If you want to process special category (sensitive) personal data, you also need to apply one of the conditions in Article 9(2). 'Explicit consent' is one option for legitimizing the use of special category data.

Consent can also legitimize restricted processing, and explicit consent can legitimize automated decision-making (including profiling), or overseas transfers by private-sector organizations in the absence of adequate safeguards.

If you rely on consent, this will affect individuals' rights. People will generally have stronger rights when processing is based on consent – for example, the right to erasure (also known as 'the right to be forgotten') and the right to data portability.

But be careful, if you are not really giving a choice, then claiming that you have consent may be wrong. Do not aim to obtain consent unless you are sure that the data subject really has a choice.

For example:

A company that provides credit cards asks its customers to give consent for their personal data to be sent to credit reference agencies for credit scoring.

However, if a customer refuses or withdraws their consent, the credit card company will still send the data to the credit reference agencies on the basis of 'legitimate interests'. So, asking for consent is misleading and inappropriate – there is no real choice. The company should have relied on 'legitimate interests' from the start. To ensure fairness and transparency, the company should still tell customers this will happen, but this is very different from giving them a choice."

If you are using consent as the basis for processing, you must make sure that it has been freely given.

Consent is defined in Article 4(11) as:

Any freely given, specific, informed and unambiguous indication of the data subject's wishes by which he or she, by a statement or by a clear affirmative action, signifies agreement to the processing of personal data relating to him or her.

Article 7(4) says:

When assessing whether consent is freely given, utmost account shall be taken of whether... the performance of a contract, including the provision of a service, is conditional on consent to the processing of personal data that is not necessary for the performance of that contract.

Recital 43 says:

Consent is presumed not to be freely given... if the performance of a contract, including the provision of a service, is dependent on the consent despite such consent not being necessary for such performance.

So, consent can be very useful but only if there is a real choice. If you have difficulty justifying "consent" as your lawful basis for processing, look at another justification. Article 6 of the GDPR lets you process personal data if there is:

- *A contract with the individual: for example, to supply goods or services they have requested, or to fulfil your obligations under an employment contract. This also includes steps taken at their request before entering into a contract.*
- *Compliance with a legal obligation: if you are required by UK or EU law to process the data for a particular purpose, you can.*
- *Vital interests: you can process personal data if it's necessary to protect someone's life. This could be the life of the data subject or someone else.*
- *A public task: if you need to process personal data to carry out your official functions or a task in the public interest – and you have a legal basis for the processing under UK law – you can. If you are a UK public authority, our view is that this is likely to give you a lawful basis for many if not all of your activities.*
- *Legitimate interests: if you are a private-sector organization, you can process personal data without consent if you have a genuine and legitimate reason (including commercial benefit), unless this is outweighed by harm to the individual's rights and interests.*

Private-sector and charitable organizations will often be able to consider the 'legitimate interests' basis in Article 6(1)(f) if they find it hard to meet the standard for consent and no other specific basis applies. This recognizes that you may have good reason to process someone's personal data without their consent – but you must ensure there is no unwarranted impact on them, and that you are still fair, transparent and accountable.

Public bodies cannot generally rely on 'legitimate interests' under the GDPR but should be able to consider the 'public task' basis in Article 6(1)(e) instead. However, you will need to be able to justify why the processing is necessary to carry out your functions – in essence, that it is proportionate and there is no less intrusive alternative. And, as always, you will need to ensure you are fair, transparent and accountable. Note that this basis cannot apply if you are acting for purposes other than your official functions – for example, if you are a hybrid body. In such circumstances you could still consider 'legitimate interests' as a potential basis, as long as the processing is otherwise lawful. (ICO)

Lawfulness of processing special categories of data

Article 9 states that you must have or know that:

1. *you have the explicit consent of the data subject, unless reliance on consent is prohibited by Member State law;*
2. *processing is necessary for carrying out obligations under employment, social security or social protection law, or a collective agreement;*
3. *processing is necessary to protect the vital interests of the data subject or another individual where the data subject is physically or legally incapable of giving consent;*
4. *processing is carried out by a not-for-profit body with a political, philosophical, religious, or trade union aim, provided the processing relates only to members or former members (or those who have regular contact with it for those purposes) and provided there is no disclosure to a third party without consent;*
5. *processing relates to information manifestly made public by the data subject;*
6. *processing is necessary for the establishment, exercise or defence of a legal claim, or where a court is acting in its judicial capacity;*
7. *processing is necessary for reasons of substantial public interest on the basis of Union or Member State law which is proportionate to the aim pursued and which contains appropriate safeguards;*
8. *processing is necessary for the purposes of preventative or occupational medicine for assessing the working capacity of employee, medical diagnosis, the provision of health or social care treatment or management of health or social care systems and services on the basis of Union or Member State law or a contract with a health professional;*
9. *processing is necessary for reasons of public interest in the area of public health, such as protecting against serious cross-border threats;*
10. *processing is necessary for archiving purposes in the public interest, or scientific and historical research purposes in accordance with Article 89(1).*

Consent

Overview

Article 4 of the GDPR deals with definitions used within the Regulation. Item 11 states:

> *consent of the data subject means any freely given, specific, informed and* **unambiguous** *indication of the data subject's wishes by which he or she,* **by a statement or by a clear affirmative action**, *signifies agreement to the processing of personal data relating to him or her"* (our emphasis)

The GDPR sets a high standard for consent.

- *Doing consent well should put individuals in control, build customer trust and engagement, and enhance your reputation.*
- *Check your consent practices and your existing consents. Refresh consents if they don't meet the GDPR standard.*
- *Consent means offering individuals genuine choice and control.*
- *Consent requires a positive opt-in. Don't use pre-ticked boxes or any other method of consent by default.*
- *Explicit consent requires a very clear and specific statement of consent.*
- *Keep your consent requests separate from other terms and conditions.*
- *Be specific and granular. Vague or blanket consent is not enough.*
- *Be clear and concise.*
- *Name any third parties who will rely on the consent.*
- *Make it easy for people to withdraw consent and tell them how.*
- *Keep evidence of consent – who, when, how, and what you told people.*
- *Keep consent under review and refresh it if anything changes.*
- *Avoid making consent a precondition of a service.*
- *Public authorities and employers will find using consent difficult.*
- *Remember – you don't always need consent. If consent is too difficult, look at whether another lawful basis is more appropriate.*

The definition of consent is similar to that in the old Data Protection Act (DPA) but the GDPR goes further. Consent must be freely given, specific, informed, and there must be for a specific purpose. If you have consent to use a data subject's personal data to run a competition, for example, then once the competition is over, you can't use that consent to run another competition. So, you have informed consent for a "specific purpose" but not for any other.

The consent must be unambiguous so that the data subject knew exactly what they were consenting to. Consent is indicated by a data subject action. That is, they have ticked a box, or requested something. You can't pre-tick a box or include the consent as a condition of something. You need to have the consent of the data subject and you must record and retain this.

Can we carry on using existing Data Protection Act (DPA) consents?

You are not required to automatically "repaper" or refresh existing DPA consents as part of your GDPR project. However, it's important to check your processes and records in detail to be sure existing consents meet the GDPR standard.

Recital 171 of the GDPR makes clear you can continue to rely on any existing consent that was given in line with the GDPR requirements, and there's no need to seek fresh consent. However, you will need to be confident that your consent requests already met the GDPR standard and that consents are properly documented. You will also need to put in place compliant mechanisms for individuals to withdraw their consent easily.

On the other hand, if existing DPA consents don't meet the GDPR's high standards or are poorly documented, you will need to seek fresh GDPR-compliant consent, identify a different lawful basis for your processing (and ensure continued processing is fair), or stop the processing.

If you rely on consent, this will also affect individuals' rights. People will generally have stronger rights when processing is based on consent – for example, *the right to erasure* (also known as "the right to be forgotten") and the *right to data portability*.

Here is a consent checklist that the ICO has provided in their "Guide to the General Data Protection Regulation (GDPR)" 08 February 2018:

Asking for consent

- *We have checked that consent is the most appropriate lawful basis for processing.*
- *We have made the request for consent prominent and separate from our terms and conditions.*
- *We ask people to positively opt in.*
- *We don't use pre-ticked boxes, or any other type of consent by default.*
- *We use clear, plain language that is easy to understand.*
- *We specify why we want the data and what we're going to do with it.*
- *We give granular options to consent to independent processing operations.*
- *We have named our organization and any third parties.*
- *We tell individuals they can withdraw their consent.*
- *We ensure that the individual can refuse to consent without detriment.*
- *We don't make consent a precondition of a service.*
- *If we offer online services directly to children, we only seek consent if we have age-verification and parental-consent measures in place.*

Recording consent

- *We keep a record of when and how we got consent from the individual.*
- *We keep a record of exactly what they were told at the time.*

Managing consent

- *We regularly review consents to check that the relationship, the processing and the purposes have not changed.*
- *We have processes in place to refresh consent at appropriate intervals, including any parental consents.*
- *We consider using privacy dashboards or other preference-management tools as a matter of good practice.*

- *We make it easy for individuals to withdraw their consent at any time and publicize how to do so.*
- *We act on withdrawals of consent as soon as we can.*
- *We don't penalize individuals who wish to withdraw consent.*

By using these checklists, you should be able to see whether you really have "consent" or not. If you need to take action to improve your methods of obtaining consent, this is a good time to review your processes.

Transferring data outside of the EU

If your organization or a supplier that you use transfers personal data outside of the EU, then you must ensure that the data is protected to the same degree as specified in the GDPR. If the country where the data will be held is not recognized as compliant with the GDPR, then you will need to ensure that you have a contract with the company that is covered by the Binding Corporate Rule, as shown above.

Defensive data

Many companies that sell data for marketing purposes will try to protect their data by inserting false records into their files. This is a very old method and dates from the time when companies bought and sold mailing lists of potential customers. Before the Internet and automated systems these lists were worth a great deal of money so the companies that had compiled them needed to protect their intellectual property. They did this by planting "false" records into a list of thousands of legitimate records. This would enable them to identify when a mailing list had been sold in breach of their confidentiality clause in their contract.

These "false records" work by sitting within the many legitimate records and if a marketing company sends an email or text or makes a phone call to one of the planted records, the owner of the original data will know that their data has been compromised and also know where the data came from.

It is a wise precaution to design your own systems to include false records where you have used an accommodation address, a separate email and even a phone number that will be answered by an answering service or even go to a separate direct dial number within your company. If you find that the records have been used, you will know that your security has been breached and can launch an investigation.

Using such a system will allow you to include a few false records in data that you send to a supplier, so that if any of the false records are contacted, you will know that the security of a particular supplier has been breached or your data has been illegally sold. Of course, it is important that you maintain a secure record of which supplier has which defensive records, so that you will be in a strong position to investigate the source of a security failure.

To create "defensive records" you will need a name, address, email, and possibly a mobile and land line number.

Names can be made up and an address can be rented from one of the many companies that hire out accommodation addresses or you may have a building that you can use. Let's say that you have an address of 123 High Street, Someville, Englandshire. You can then create records for Flat1, Flat 2, 3 etc. and generate many records for a single "real" address. You can then either create a web-address that you can use to generate email addresses or use one of the free email providers. And if you need a phone number to make the record look legitimate, you can use a block of pay-as-you-go mobile phones. Of course, you will need to test the postal and email addresses from time to time to make sure you are receiving messages.

This may seem like a lot of work but if there is a security breach it will be very helpful to know where the breach occurred. On the other hand, if there seems to have been a large-scale security breach with customers being contacted but where none of your defensive records have been sent a message, you may start to suspect that the breach occurred at a different supplier and take action to identify the real source of the leak and thereby protect your own reputation and prevent your company from being falsely accused of being the source of the data loss.

There is one other reason for doing this. If you are accused of losing customer data, you could be liable to a substantial fine but under the GDPR, you can also be sued for damages and this can be a game changer for many companies. It can be hard to prove a negative, like trying to "prove" that your security has not been compromised but if you have strong defences, good audit records *and* can show that none of your defensive data addresses have been contacted, you may well be able to prove you are innocent and clear your name.

Data protection by design and default

The GDPR states (Article 25(2)):

The controller shall implement appropriate technical and organizational measures for ensuring that, by default, only personal data which are necessary for each specific purpose of the processing are processed. That obligation applies to the amount of personal data collected, the extent of their processing, the period of their storage and their accessibility. In particular, such measures shall ensure that by default personal data are not made accessible without the individual's intervention to an indefinite number of natural persons.

In practice, what this means is that, as part of compliance, appropriate security and businesses practices must be in place to ensure that security of personal and if applicable sensitive data is at the forefront of any action or reaction to a new business venture, change of operation, new software or service or indeed anything else that may have an effect on personal data. In short, the GDPR is stating that the security of personal data must be embedded into a business such that it is just second nature.

Section
9
Data breaches

Penalties

There are two levels of fines: security breach, that causes an infringement of any of the Article 8, 11, 25–39, 41(4), 42 or 43 shall be subject to an administrative fine of up to €10m or up to 2% of the world-wide annual turnover of the previous year, whichever is the higher.

An infringement of any of the Articles 5, 6, 7, 9, 12–22, 44–49, 58(2) and any obligations pursuant to State Law under Chapter IX (Articles 85–91) shall be subject to a fine of up to €20m or 4% of the world-wide annual turnover of the previous year.

Now it is worth pointing out that these penalties are for a worst-case breach but they are punitive and they are meant to act as a deterrent. The level of fine imposed in the UK under previous DPA legislation could be seen to influence security budget investment decisions. This is no longer the case and a company that deliberately ignores the requirement of the GDPR could find that they are facing a fine at the upper end of the scale. You should also note that Article 83 (1) states "Each supervisory authority shall ensure that the imposition of administrative fines pursuant to this Article in respect of infringements of this Regulation referred to in paragraphs 4, 5 and 6 shall in each individual case be effective, proportionate and dissuasive." So, while a serious breach of the Regulation may result in a fine that will hurt, it is not intended to cause the organization so much damage that the organization can no longer function. However, it will be up to the judgement of the relevant SA to determine the level of any fine.

Compensation

In addition to a possible fine, there is another danger. Article 82(1) states

> Any person who has suffered material or non-material damage as a result of an infringement of this Regulation shall have the right to receive compensation from the controller or processor for the damage suffered.

The UK Data Protection Act of 2018 has been brought into line with the GDPR. Two notable clauses of the DPA2018 are Clauses 168 and 169 which state:

Clause 168: **Compensation for contravention of the GDPR**

1. *In Article 82 of the GDPR (right to compensation for material or non-material damage), "non-material damage" includes distress.*
2. *Subsection (3) applies where—*

    (a) *in accordance with rules of court, proceedings under Article 82 of the GDPR are brought by a representative body on behalf of a person, and*
    (b) *a court orders the payment of compensation.*

3. *the court may make an order providing for the compensation to be paid on behalf of the person to—*

    (a) *the representative body, or*
    (b) *such other person as the court thinks fit.*

Clause 169: **Compensation for contravention of other data protection legislation**

1. *A person who suffers damage by reason of a contravention of a requirement of the data protection legislation, other than the GDPR, is entitled to compensation for that damage from the controller or the processor, subject to subsections (2) and (3).*
2. *Under subsection (1)—*

    (a) *a controller involved in processing of personal data is liable for any damage caused by the processing, and*
    (b) *a processor involved in processing of personal data is liable for damage caused by the processing only if the processor—*

    (i) *has not complied with an obligation under the data protection legislation specifically directed at processors, or*
    (ii) *has acted outside, or contrary to, the controller's lawful instructions.*

3. *A controller or processor is not liable as described in subsection (2) if the controller or processor proves that the controller or processor is not in any way responsible for the event giving rise to the damage.*

4. *A joint controller in respect of the processing of personal data to which Part 3 or 4 applies whose responsibilities are determined in an arrangement under section 58 or 104 is only liable as described in subsection (2) if the controller is responsible for compliance with the provision of the data protection legislation that is contravened.*

5. *In this section, "damage" includes financial loss and damage not involving financial loss, such as distress.*

There is a real fear that the compensation culture may spread into the world of the GDPR and the current breed of "ambulance chasers" will become European-wide "data chasers" where small amounts of compensation are claimed for minor infringements of the Regulation. As the Regulation matures and case law clarifies what can be claimed for, the situation may become clearer. We may also see an attempt to bring cases to UK courts if geographic jurisdiction is ambiguous.

Breaches

There are rules governing what breaches you must report to a supervisory authority. You may also need to inform the data subjects that their data has possibly been accessed. Article 33, subsection 1 states:

In the case of a personal data breach, the controller shall without undue delay and, where feasible, not later than 72 hours after having become aware of it, notify the personal data breach to the supervisory authority competent in accordance with Article 55, unless the personal data breach is unlikely to result in a risk to the rights and freedoms of natural persons. Where the notification to the supervisory authority is not made within 72 hours, it shall be accompanied by reasons for the delay.

So how is a breach defined?

Article 4 defines the terms used in the GDPR and subsection 12 states:

'personal data breach' means a breach of security leading to the accidental or unlawful destruction, loss, alteration, unauthorized disclosure of, or access to, personal data transmitted, stored or otherwise processed;

The definition of a personal data breach is quite wide and would cover the situation, for example, where your systems were infected with a virus that encrypted your data. While the criminal doesn't have your data, neither do you and the destruction would need to be reported to your SA.

A data breach means a failure of security leading to:

* the accidental disclosure of
* unauthorized destruction of
* loss of

- alteration of
- unauthorized disclosure to
- or access to

personal data.

You need to make sure that your internal controls are fit for purpose, your perimeter security is working, your anti-virus measures are functioning correctly and that your staff know not to put personal data at risk. You will also need to ensure that your systems are monitored and checked on a regular basis.

Do you need to notify the SA about all data breaches?

You only have to notify the relevant SA of a breach where it is likely to result in an ongoing or future risk to the rights and freedoms of individuals. If unaddressed such a breach is likely to have a significant detrimental effect on individuals – for example, result in discrimination, damage to reputation, financial loss, loss of confidentiality or any other significant economic or social disadvantage.

This has to be assessed on a case by case basis. For example, you will need to notify the relevant SA about a loss of customer details where the breach leaves individuals open to identity theft. On the other hand, the loss or inappropriate alteration of a staff telephone list, for example, would not normally meet this threshold.

Clearly there will be many possible breaches in between these two clear cases but we would urge you to exercise caution and report a breach if you are in any doubt. Stating that you need to look at the nature of the breach is a simple thing to write but in practice you may be very unsure about exactly what has happened and how it occurred.

In our earlier example of a virus encrypting your customer data, would you need to report it? If you have good backups and can recover the data, then there has not been any loss of facilities, you probably don't need to report it. However, where the virus has destroyed your data and you do not have a backup that is clean, then you should report this

Of importance when dealing with a reportable breach is timeliness and how effective your processes are. General staff awareness is essential so that when an issue arises time is not lost escalating it to the DPO, investigating and reporting to the SA. You may for example want to set some internal guiding targets such as:

(a) 24hrs: issue reported to DPO and provisional assessment review held
(b) 48hrs: issues determined to be a breach and/or reportable. Draft breach submission completed. Data subjects notified.
(c) 32hrs: final review and confirmation to/not to report made.
(d) 36hrs: other regulatory bodies notified.

Incident response plan

Larger organizations will generally have in place an incident response plan or incident management process. If your business doesn't have a process then it is advisable to consider defining a process that can be followed by your employees. Irrespective of whether or not you decide or need to report a data breach any such incident should be recorded, not least because if the same incident or similar takes place at a later date, you will have a record of your actions which will assist your process management and also indicate to your SA, in the event of an inquiry, that you take incidents seriously.

The best plans or processes are those that can be easily followed. It is important that, at the outset of an incident, just one person is in control and manages those people who have been drafted-in to assist.

Events leading to the incident need to be clarified and logged and then actions in managing the incident also need to be logged. There should be no assumptions made, just the known facts. If the incident is reported to your SA then this must be recorded in detail and any subsequent communication with affected parties must be recorded.

Who should be involved?

The fewer the people involved the better and those involved will be dependent too on the type of incident. If, for example, the breach is a result of an external cyber-attack, then those involved would typically include the person reporting the incident or breach, the security manager, the DPO (or person responsible for data management), the head of IT and depending on the severity, the COO or even CEO. If the breach is due to internal malpractice, then your head of HR might also be involved. Once your core team has been identified and mobilized then each member of that team may have sub-teams to carry out dedicated investigation.

What is most important is that the nominated incident manager receives only pertinent facts from the person in his or her team responsible for their area of expertise.

Victim or villain?

Any system that is not subject to regular monitoring is likely to be at risk. If the worst does happen, will the general public and your customers see you as a victim or villain?

Suppose you read that a 15-year-old schoolboy downloaded a script from the Internet and managed to bypass your security because you hadn't bothered to install a security patch that had been available for six months. In addition, you didn't realize that this child had been accessing your systems most evenings for the past month. You will probably feel that the company has been so lax with their security that they are almost responsible for the crime.

If, on the other hand, you read that a gang of professional criminals had charged into a local bank branch and shown the hollow end of a sawn-off shotgun to a young bank clerk and walked out with several thousand pounds, you will probably feel that the bank is a victim of a vicious criminal gang.

The truth is that both companies may have had a failure of security. The victim of the hacker may have been unable to apply the patch because of a systems incompatibility with the upgrade and the bank may have been a soft touch because they had become complacent, but the newspaper headlines will probably show more sympathy to the bank than to the hacking victim.

In any event, if you are the victim of a hacker but manage to see what they are doing and prevent a serious data loss, you will be in a much better position to face your customers and senior management than if you didn't notice that you were being attacked.

Monitoring

There are many good products that allow you to monitor your systems and to be aware of any security alerts. Accidents do happen and data can become corrupted; the real sin is to be unaware that it has happened. Your system should have several layers of defence that can act as a deterrent and as an alarm. If your organization is deemed more vulnerable to an external threat then you might consider the installation of a Security Incident Event Management system (SIEM) which will provide you with customized alerts of cyber activity.

Perimeter

You should protect your perimeter in one or more of a number of ways. Your network should have a Firewall, or probably a set of Firewall pairs to divide your network into a public, and untrusted portion, a partially trusted section and a trusted portion where your main systems and data exist. With this sort of design, a hacker will need to bypass several layers of your security.

Within your network you should be looking for any unauthorized access attempts and this can be achieved by using an intrusion detection system, an intrusion prevention system (that is actively trying to defend your systems and network) and report on any anomalies that it detects.

Then you can actively monitor your customer data by using a Data Loss Prevention (DLP) System to check who does what with your data. You will have employees who need to have access to your data in order to do their job. They may need to be able to correct data that is wrong and delete files that are corrupt. However, they will not need to be able to copy vast amounts of customer data and write this onto an external drive. There are systems on the market that will monitor and report so that authorized staff can work as needed but a rogue employee should be prevented from extracting data that they do not have a valid reason to access. Many hackers will try to use an existing "valid" use account to extract data (see below). With a good DLP in place, there is a good chance that the hacker will be prevented from removing much data and the security team should be able to identify what data they did copy.

Security testing

Security testing comes in two main forms. There are automated scripts that will look for known vulnerabilities and report if it looks like your systems are vulnerable. At a deeper level you can look at penetration testing. This can be very effective at seeing if a possible weakness can be exploited. This is where you hire a consultant to try to breach your security and there are two main ways that they can do this.

Unauthorized attack. This is where you use a consultant but give them no access to your systems (they will be "authorized" to try to bypass your security but you don't give them any special access). They are simulating the way that a general hacker would attack your systems.

Authorized attack. This is where you hire a consultant to attack your systems but give them access to part of it. If you operate a website where you allow your customers to log-in, you should use an authorized attack to see if a customer can break out of the security envelope that you have them in.

Section
10

Your technology environment

Introduction

The systems that you use to interact with your customers are likely to be in the form of a website, apps or use contact centre technology, but these are unlikely to be the only system that you use. You need to ensure that any system you use to collect and/or process personal data is GDPR-compliant by design.

Website

You probably use a website to promote your business, indeed you may well use a website as "your business" but you may also use social media. If you use these systems to collect personal data they will be in-scope of the GDPR and you will be responsible for the personal data that you store on them. If possible, it is better to use social media as a marketing and awareness platform that directs people to your website than it is to use them as a data collection point.

If you entrust your data to social media systems you are in danger of losing control of where it is stored. Responding to a "right to be forgotten" instruction could put you in a more difficult position than would be the case if you owned the storage platforms. You may want to review any use of social media to collect data in order to reduce problems later on. In any case you must be sure that you "own" your customer data. If you are using any of the social media platforms for data collection, check to see if you own the data and where the data is stored, backed up and how you can access it.

Intranet

Do you use an intranet within your organization and do you allow your staff to use this system to input their data? If so, you will have to treat this as a data collection point with the necessary privacy statements that tell your staff what you will do with the data.

Extranet

If you have an Extranet then you will be allowing external access into your network. Aside from the fact that you are introducing a vulnerability into your network, which must be carefully monitored, you will potentially be allowing authorized organizations to access your data and possible unauthorized access to personal data. It is imperative, therefore, that you have adequate access control in place.

Mobile apps

Many organizations have mobile apps in addition to or instead of a traditional website. The use of mobile apps can allow you to extend your business but you need to recognize the additional risks to your data and your reputation.

Social media

Personal data exists on some social media sites. That is a fact of life. However, if you are using social media as a business enabler then you will have to be extremely careful that your employees (most probably HR and Marketing) are aware that they may potentially be dealing with personal data and will have to know how to handle the same to ensure privacy.

On-line file sharing

On-line file sharing is a simple way to move large amounts of data between organizations and personnel. There are numerous file sharing systems available for free but beware! Using a free application to move data may result in the loss of intellectual property rights for your data. There is also a high likelihood that it is misused by your employees resulting in data leakage, data loss and/or data theft which of course will result in a data breach. If you are going to use a proprietary file sharing system then always purchase a licence. This way you will be in control of who transmits data and how, when and what data is transmitted.

Bring your own device – BYOD

Many organizations now permit employees to use their personal devices for work. If your organization does so then ensure that you have a robust BYOD policy in place. It would be a simple matter for an employee to inadvertently or maliciously copy data, including personal and/or sensitive, to their own device which is the of course removed from the office environment. BYOD is the bane of many security managers as it makes control of data very difficult. One effective use of BYOD is to insist that any employee using their own device for work must access company data via a controlled medium, for example, VPN or by running a thin-client emulator. This way, all data will remain on the company servers and cannot be moved to the personal device.

Backend systems

People naturally think of "customer data" when considering the GDPR and will often see this as being collected by a website. However, if you have employees you may well have backend systems. Your accounts, HR system, employee tracking and monitoring system (that is used for performance reviews, training, career-planning, holidays and sickness) will hold personal data. If your employees provide input to this system, say in the form of a time-sheet, then you should provide them with a privacy statement when they use it. You will also need to ensure that you can identify what data you hold in the event of a subject access request from an employee, or a former employee.

Legacy systems

In the twenty-first century there are a disturbing number of legacy systems that are processing vast amounts of data. Many of these systems still run on COBOL. If you own one of these systems, can you modify it to ensure that you comply with the GDPR? Can you amend the data fields that are being stored or change the system to provide a file of data to comply with a request for a customer data in a common portable form as required under Article 20?

Do any legacy systems that you use allow you to delete a record, or to flag it to restrict further processing if needed?

Where do you process your data?

Where you process, including where you host your website, can have a bearing on how you comply with the GDPR. If you are processing large amounts of personal data, then you may choose to have your European operation based in a data centre that is within the GDPR area. You do not need to be a large multi-billion-dollar organization to justify splitting your processing and your data storage. If the majority of your data comes from individuals that are outside of the EU, then you may have split your data processing and storage, as explained in Section 1, earlier.

Section
11

Assessing your suppliers

Assessing your suppliers for security

As a data controller you have the responsibility for ensuring that data processing activities comply with the Regulation (Article 24) and this means that you have to establish that any third-party supplier is also complying with the Regulation (Article 28).

Data is a vital part of your business and safe keeping of that data is of utmost importance in order to protect financial interests, maintain regulatory compliance, and protect company brand and reputation. Prior to releasing any data to an organization outside of your company or group, the supplier should undergo a review of their IT security which will typically include an analysis of their technical security, operational platforms, procedures and processes, documentation, or any other aspect deemed appropriate dependent upon the service to be provided. You should ask your current or potential supplier to complete a questionnaire on their security processes. This should not be over-complicated or your supplier may simply refuse to answer the questions. Indeed, a supplier who has achieved a certified level of security may just provide you with a statement. This is okay as long as they also provide you with a copy of their certificate and at least a statement from their Board of Directors.

However, you should be prepared to provide your supplier with a questionnaire and we include a typical example later in this chapter.

Key areas of security you should consider

Although aimed at your supplier, you might also consider asking such questions of your own business.

Organization

You should establish whether data is stored in countries and with companies where appropriate regulations and guidelines are applicable.

Data stored with a cloud service provider, where geographic location of the data cannot be clearly stated, should consider the reputation and size of the service provider.

- data to be stored within the UK is preferred
- data to be stored within the EU is generally acceptable to any regulators.

Data to be stored within a non-EU country that adheres to the GDPR and is on the EU list of countries that it accepts as compliant is acceptable.

- Data to be stored in any other country should be considered as a possible risk and it will be up to you to ensure that the supplier complies with the GDPR. You can do this by having a carefully worded contract that ensures that the organization will comply with the Regulation.

Payment Card Industry/Data Security Standard (PCI/DSS)

You should know if you are required to comply with the requirements of the Payment Card Industry Data Security Standards. If you don't handle any payment details at all then you can ignore the PCI/DSS requirements. If you use a payment provider, such as PayPal or WorldPay, then you need to ensure that your IT systems are PCI compliant. If in doubt, you should speak with your merchant provider to be sure.

Security policy

Do you have a documented information security policy and management system in line with external industry recognized standards such as ISO27000? Are these:

- communicated to, understood and accepted by all employees, suppliers, and agents, at time of enrolment and at regular intervals ongoing
- regularly reviewed to be kept relevant with emerging technology and threats
- supported by senior management
- inclusive of incident and change management procedures?

You should indicate accountability and segregation of duties for information security and you should also indicate, where a sub-contractor is used in the provision of the service, or where a sub-contractor is permitted access to your data, that comparative policies are maintained.

Your supplier should indicate that

- access to your data is provided on a need-only basis
- access permission allocations and revocations are auditable
- service activity and data access is auditable.

Network access controls

You should indicate that appropriate network segregation exists and that:

- development, testing and production environments are distinct and separated
- networks and systems used to provide the service are segregated from other functions
- intrusion attempts and malicious activity generate system reactions
- access from an external connection is restricted and auditable
- use of wireless networking is restricted and auditable.

Server and PC protection, physical and environmental security

You should indicate that procedures are defined for

- patch management and anti-virus updates
- secure disposal of computer equipment, digital storage media, and printed material.

You should indicate that networks and systems are protected against:

- fire
- flood
- power interruptions
- unauthorized physical access.

You should indicate that secure backup procedures are defined and that data in storage or transit is appropriately encrypted and secured.

Sample Information Security Questionnaire

(A Security Questionnaire template is available for download)

Part One: Organization, Policies & Procedures

Item	Requirement	Notes
1.0	Is there an individual member of the Senior Management Team assigned responsibility for IT Security?	Record their name, job title and contact details.
1.1	Is there a Senior Information Risk Officer (SIRO)?	Ideally there should be board-level representation for security and data.
1.2	Is there an individual responsible for data protection or a dedicated Data Protection Officer?	Record their name, job title and contact details.
1.3	Are there policies regarding Information Security and Data Protection which are reviewed at least annually?	There should be policies routinely updated and made available to all employees.
1.4	Do you have procedures to deal with Information Security Incidents and Data Breaches?	There must be guidance made available to all employees on how to recognize and deal with Information Security Incidents and Data Breaches.
1.5	Do you have procedures to deal with Subject Access Requests?	The nominated person responsible for Data Protection must know how to respond to a Subject Access Request.
1.6	Do you have a Privacy Notice?	All Data Subjects (including employees) must know how their Personal Data is collected and used and must be made aware of their individual Rights.

Part Two: Certification

Item	Requirement	Notes
2.0	Are you currently, or are you seeking compliance or certification to a recognized Information Security Standard or Framework?	This may be the internationally recognized ISO27001:2013 framework, UK-Government Cyber Essentials framework, the US Government NIST framework or any other recognized framework.
2.1	If you are processing payments for customers, are you PCI/DSS Compliant?	This data security standard is required by most banks.

Part Three: Risk Management

Item	Requirement	Notes
3.0	Have you adopted a formal Risk Management process with all identified Risks recorded in a Risk Treatment Register?	Risk Management is key to Information Security and will also support your annual DPIA.
3.1	Where identified Risks fall outside your Risk Acceptance, can you confirm that active mitigation has been or is taking place?	Any Risks that are not within the accepted levels should have appropriate mitigation recorded.

(Continued)

(*Continued*)

Part Three: Risk Management

3.2	Can you confirm that an Information Asset Register exists and that all recorded Information groups have been Risk Assessed?	It is imperative that all your Information Assets are recorded with any identified Risk, especially where Personal and Sensitive Information is recorded.
3.3	Can you confirm that Data Protection by Design and Default is embedded into your company processes?	Data Protection relies on timely and effective Risk Analysis and Treatment.

Part Four: Access Management

4.0	Are all users provided with a unique ID and password?	ID and password sharing is not acceptable within Information Security.
4.1	Can you confirm that user passwords are a minimum of eight characters alpha-numeric and are changed at least every 180 days?	Alpha-numeric passwords are stronger than easily-guessed character streams. Changing passwords regularly is highly recommended.
4.2	Can you confirm that Service and Administrative IDs are kept to a minimum and require two-factor authentication?	There should be a minimum number of service and admin IDs available. Where accounts are shared then two-factor authentication is highly recommended.
4.3	Do you use a Password database and is it hashed or encrypted?	Formal Password Management systems are highly recommended.
4.4	Are accounts locked-out after multiple attempts of access? If so, how many attempts and what is the reset process?	Typically, three failed attempts at log-in should provoke an account lock. Ideally the user must make a request in person to reset the account.
4.5	Is there a defined process for applying and revoking user accounts?	A user account should be provided with the minimum access rights for that person's role. There must be a process for revoking accounts.
4.6	Do you permit remote access to your network for employees?	Remote access should be controlled and ideally should require two-factor authentication.
4.7	Do you permit remote access for approved third-party access?	Remote access should be controlled and ideally should require two-factor authentication.
4.8	Apart from access control can you confirm that users (including by remote access) are only able to access information appropriate to their role?	Access to information should be on a 'need to know' basis and approved by the Information Owner.

Part Five: Security in Information Management

5.0	Is any Information at Rest encrypted?	Although not a strict requirement, where information is retained on portable devices, those devices are recommended to have full-disk encryption.
5.1	If Personal Data is retained on company servers, is such information Pseudonymized?	Pseudonymized data is recognized as more secure than clear text.
5.2	Are there procedures and/or facilities to protect data in transit?	Sensitive information should not be transmitted electronically unless encrypted unless over a secure link or via SFTP for example.
5.3	Do you have a defined data retention and deletion policy?	Unless legally obliged to, it is recommended that data be routinely 'weeded' and that unnecessary information be archived and/or deleted.

Part Six: Network Security

6.0	Is your network protected by at least one Firewall?	A Firewall is the first line of defence against Cyber Attack. Ideally your Firewall will have IDS and IPS enabled as added security.
6.1	Are software firewalls enabled on company laptops?	Windows ships with a software firewall that is enabled by default; ensure that this has not been disabled.
6.2	Is your network protected by at least two malware programs in addition to anti-virus protection on end-point devices?	Having two programs to combat malicious software will increase your chances of combating malware. Laptops and PC's should also have a separate AV system that is updated daily.
6.3	Are your network and end-point devices routinely scanned for vulnerabilities and patched appropriately?	Routine scanning will indicate if your network has become vulnerable to exploitable code. A large network should be scanned at least quarterly and patched every month.
6.4	Does your network and website(s) undergo regular Penetration Testing?	Unlike a vulnerability test, a Penetration test will probe your network for weaknesses that an attacker might use to gain illegal access. A Pen test should be carried out at least annually.
6.5	Do you retain logs of user/admin activity which can be reviewed?	Although it is not always practical to review logs, having them available to assist in any incident or breach management is highly recommended.

(Continued)

(Continued).

Part Seven: Environmental Security

7.0	Is physical access to your premises controlled?	The use of card or PIN systems for building/room entry is recommended. Visitors should be escorted or at least only have limited access.
7.1	Are server rooms secure?	Rooms containing networking and data storage equipment must be physically secure and have strictly controlled access.
7.2	Is physical backup media stored securely where not off-site?	Incremental backup media should be stored in a fire-proof safe and weekly/monthly backup should be stored securely off-site.
7.3	Are critical systems protected against power surges and is there provision of UPS?	Power surges and power loss can lead to compromised data; therefore, power protection is highly recommended as part of your DR and BCMS processes.
7.4	Do you have policies and procedures for the destruction of physical media?	Using a certified company for the destruction of magnetic media and confidential paper waste is highly recommended.

Section

12

Direct marketing

Introduction

There are many countries that offer their citizens similar levels of protection to those that were in place under previous EU data protection rules. However, the GDPR has raised the game and increased the rights of the citizen to a whole new level.

Marketing is a particular area where you may need to change your working practices in order to make sure you are working within the law. Bear in mind that there are now much stricter rules that you must follow if you are to avoid problems. There are two issues that you need to be aware of. Firstly, the potential penalties for failing to comply with the GDPR/DPA 2018 are very much harsher than they were under previous legislation that was in force before the GDPR. Secondly there is now the option for a data subject who has been wronged to sue for compensation. In addition to the GDPR you must also follow the PECR, the Privacy and Electronic Communications (EC Directive). This Regulation was originally passed in 2003 and has been amended several times since.

With the introduction of data subjects being able to claim compensation, some consultants fear that this is an area where the unscrupulous "ambulance chasers" will be looking to make easy money and we can expect the whiplash and PPI claim adverts to be replaced with "Have you suffered at the hands of a marketing company?" Only time will tell if this becomes a problem area but the safest way to avoid potential problems is to make sure you comply with the Regulation.

Direct marketing

While there is not a definition of direct marketing within the GDPR, a reasonable working definition would be: "Electronic communications sent between particular parties over a phone line or the Internet with a view to promoting an organization or product. This includes phone calls, faxes, text messages, video messages, emails and Internet messaging."

This will be specific information and not be generally available information as would be found on a website or in an advert that has been placed for general viewing or listening such as one placed in a magazine, on a billboard or on a TV, film or radio programme.

Within this book we are limiting ourselves to messages that have been sent to an individual. There are other rules that cover corporate communications that are aimed at a company. Here we are looking at marketing that is aimed at an individual or individuals. These rules cover any marketing, not just commercial marketing so material that is promoting the aims of a charity, political party, or a religious organization will be included.

Market research

These rules do not cover genuine market research, i.e. calls that are conducted to discover opinion, for example. Provided that the purpose of the call is for genuine research purposes and does not go on to promote a specific product or service or to gather data for later marketing purposes, these calls are excluded from the legislation.

Consent

Before you can send direct marketing material to an individual or individuals, you must have their consent. A reasonable working definition of consent is

"Any freely given specific, informed indication of her or his wishes by which she or he signifies their agreement to having their personal data processed for this purpose."

This consent does not have to be by way of a website but may be more general. The goldfish bowl is a good example. Most of us will be familiar with attending conferences and seminars where there is a goldfish bowl and you are invited to drop in your business card. At the end of the event a winning card will be drawn out and there will be a winner of the prize. Commonly, all but one of the entries will be sent an email telling them that they haven't won the prize and asking them if they are interested in the sponsor's product. This will be illegal under the GDPR. It will almost certainly be acceptable to inform the people that they have not won the prize, as consent was implicit in them placing their business card in the bowl for this purpose but to then market them will be wrong. You must have clear and unambiguous consent in order to market.

The GDPR says what the law intends to do but there is no case law at the time of writing, so we are working on the wording of the Regulation. The PECR has been around for much longer but as it is closely linked to the GDPR it will be wise to look for early cases that test the legislation.

Implied consent

In general consent must be explicit, as would be the case if you ask a potential customer to fill in a form on your website and asked them to tick a box if they agree to being sent marketing information. There are times when implied consent will be acceptable for use of personal data. If you fill in a form asking for a product to be sent to you, it is reasonable to assume that you have given consent to use the name and address to post the parcel. Implied consent is very unlikely to be acceptable for marketing purposes.

Please be aware that this is in relation to the marketing of adults; marketing children will require far more caution and will be dealt with separately.

Children

Children are given special protection in a number of areas within the GDPR and marketing is no exception. Recital 38 states:

Children merit specific protection with regard to their personal data, as they may be less aware of the risks, consequences and safeguards concerned and their rights in relation to the processing of personal data. Such specific protection should, in particular, apply to the use of personal data of children for the purposes of marketing or creating personality or user profiles and the collection of personal data with regard to children when using services offered directly to a child. The consent of the holder of parental responsibility should not be necessary in the context of preventive or counselling services offered directly to a child.

All children must be told anything in plain English and in language that they can understand given their age. If you are marketing children, be aware that children under 13 years of age get even more protection and can't enter into a contract. Article 8 of the GDPR looks at age. It states:

Where point (a) of Article 6(1) applies, in relation to the offer of information society services directly to a child, the processing of the personal data of a child shall be lawful where the child is at least 16 years old. Where the child is below the age of 16 years, such processing shall be lawful only if and to the extent that consent is given or authorized by the holder of parental responsibility over the child. Member States may provide by law for a lower age for those purposes provided that such lower age is not below 13 years.

Please note that if you are dealing with children from a number of EU countries, you may need to take the safest option and assume that no child under the age of 16 may give consent without the approval of a responsible adult.

Telephone and text marketing

In addition to being sure that you have consent to market via email or letter, you will also need consent before you can call or text people for marketing purposes. Just as consent may be withdrawn at any time, there is another route that people may use to block marketing calls and texts. Many European countries operate a telephone preference service so that a consumer may register their number and it then becomes illegal to call them for marketing purposes. Some countries will also have a fax and a mailing preference services. When you are considering a direct marketing campaign in Europe, you will be wise to check whether the country operates any form of marketing preference service. If they do, you should check to see if any of your phone numbers are listed and if they are, you must remove the details from your list of people to contact.

Lists

It is very common for many to buy in marketing lists and also to sell lists that they have built. Under the GDPR/PECR this becomes much harder to do. If you do buy in a list it is very important to ensure that the company you are buying from is reputable and that you have a well-worded contract with them.

Before considering if you can sell a list of your customers, you must ensure that they have agreed to having their details sold and also agreed to them being sold to a company in the sector that you are considering selling to. Selling data is much harder under the GDPR/PECR. Having said that, it does mean that any data that can be sold will be much more valuable than was the case in the past, so as with so many things, there is a balance to be struck.

Example

In 2018 a British political consulting firm, Cambridge Analytica, was accused of poor practices after it was reported in the media that it had acquired and used personal data about Facebook users which it had obtained from an external researcher who had advised Facebook he was collecting it for academic purposes. The mistake was on the part of Cambridge Analytica and the seller of the data not checking that the data subjects were aware of the use of their data. This led the UK Information Commissioners Office to obtain a warrant to search Cambridge Analytica's servers and a ban by Facebook from advertising on its servers. In May of 2018 Cambridge Analytica and its parent company filed for insolvency proceedings and closed operations.

Profiling

In Article 4(4), the GDPR states:

'profiling' means any form of automated processing of personal data consisting of the use of personal data to evaluate certain personal aspects relating to a natural person, in particular to analyze or predict aspects concerning that natural person's performance at work, economic situation, health, personal preferences, interests, reliability, behavior, location or movements

Profiling is often used to identify people based on their traits, preferences and expected traits and preferences. Targeted adverts based on profiling is widespread and very effective as is the use of profiling in criminal investigations and prevention (by identifying what an individual is likely to do in the future).

Because of the power of profiling when used with data taken from various sources, the GDPR mentions profiling 11 times within the Articles and 12 times in the Recitals. If you use profiling of individuals for targeted marketing you will need to ensure that you are open and transparent with them. In particular your privacy statement(s) must be clear.

In particular, Article 22 states

The data subject shall have the right not to be subject to a decision based solely on automated processing, including profiling, which produces legal effects concerning him or her or similarly significantly affects him or her.

See Article 22 in Section 14 for the full wording.

Summary

Here is an example checklist for marketing purposes. The ICO has more information on checklists including interactive forms for marketing.

Obtaining consent for marketing

- *We use opt-in boxes*
- *We specify methods of communication (e.g. by email, text, phone, recorded call, post)*
- *We ask for consent to pass details to third parties for marketing and name, or clearly describe those third parties*
- *We record when and how we got consent, and exactly what it covers*

Bought in lists – General

- *We check that the seller is a member of a professional body (or is accredited in some way)*
- *We don't use bought-in lists for texts, emails or recorded calls (unless we have proof of opt-in consent within last six months which specifically named or clearly described us)*
- *The product, service or ideals we are marketing are the same or similar to those that the individuals originally consented to receive marketing for*
- *We only use the information on the lists for marketing purposes*
- *We delete any irrelevant or excessive personal information*
- *We screen the names on bought-in lists against our own list of people who say they don't want our calls (suppression list)*
- *We carry out small sampling exercises to assess the reliability of the data on the lists*
- *We have procedures for dealing with inaccuracies and complaints.*
- *When marketing by post, email or fax we include our company name, address and telephone number in the content*
- *We tell people where we obtained their details*
- *We provide people with a privacy notice (where it is practicable to do so)*
- *We tie the seller into a contract which confirms the reliability of the list and gives us the ability to audit*

The seller can verify that the people on the list:

- *gave specific consent to receive marketing from us (or a clearly defined category of organizations fitting our description);*
- *were provided with readily accessible, clear and intelligible information about how their contact details would be used (e.g. privacy notices were easy to find and understand);*
- *were offered a clear and genuine choice whether or not to have their details used for marketing purposes;*
- *took positive action to indicate their consent (e.g. ticked a box, clicked a button or subscribed to a service);*
- *gave their consent reasonably recently (within the last six months); and*
- *in the case of texts, emails or automated calls, gave specific consent to receive marketing by those means.*

Marketing by mail

- *We have screened the names and addresses against the Mail Preference Service*
- *The individuals on the list have at least given a general statement that they are happy to receive marketing from us*
- *Where the individuals haven't given specific consent, marketing is consistent with the context in which the information was provided and concerns a similar product, service or ideal*

Live calls

- *We screen the numbers against the Telephone Preference Service (TPS) (or for corporate subscribers the Corporate Telephone Preference Service (CTPS))*
- *We keep our own do-not-call list of anyone who says they don't want our calls*
- *We screen against our do-not-call list*
- *We display our number to the person we're calling*

Automated calls

- *We only make recorded calls where we have opt-in consent*
- *We display our number to the person we're calling*

Marketing by email or text

- *We only text or email with opt-in consent (unless contacting previous customers about our own similar products, and we offered them an opt-out when they gave their details)*
- *We offer an opt-out (by reply or unsubscribe link)*
- *We keep a list of anyone who opts out*
- *We screen against our opt-out list*

Faxes

- *The individuals on the list have specifically consented to receiving marketing faxes from us*
- *We have screened their numbers against the Fax Preference Service (FPS)*

Section

13

Privacy Notice(s)

Your Privacy Notice(s) is an area where the GDPR and previous data protection legislation vary a great deal. Please remember that the Privacy Notice refers to the personal data that you hold and or process. It is not just the data that you are collecting through your website or social media, even though that is where you are most likely to be publishing your Privacy Notice. You must think about *all* of the data that you are using.

Articles 12, 13 and 14 of the GDPR outline the requirements that need to be taken into account when providing your privacy information to data subjects. The GDPR requires you to provide information that is:

- concise, clear and easy to understand
- written in plain language
- if addressed to a child, uses terminology that they will be familiar with
- free of charge.

Article 12 deals with the rights of the data subject to access their data and your duty to comply with a request and gives the time-scale that you must meet.

Article 13 looks at what information you need to provide if the information came from the data subject and Article 14 looks at what information you will need to provide if your data came from any other source than the data subject. While these Articles tell you what information is needed to be provided to the data subject, they don't tell you where to provide this information so you will need to look at your existing privacy notices and see if they are still fit for purpose.

Your privacy notice(s) should explain what you do in terms of the principles of the GDPR. These are explained in detail in Article 5 and are that your data will be:

1. processed lawfully and fairly
2. collected for specific legitimate purposes

3. adequate, relevant and limited to what is necessary
4. accurate and will be kept up-to-date
5. kept for no longer than is necessary
6. kept securely.

Your privacy notice(s) also need to explain the lawful basis for the collection and processing and the lawful ways that you can collect data are:

a. the data subject has given permission
b. processing is necessary for complying with a contract
c. processing is necessary for complying with a legal obligation
d. processing is necessary for complying with a law
e. processing is necessary for carrying out a task that is in the public interest
f. processing is in your legitimate interests.

When designing your privacy notices, you should consider where you are collecting the data. If you are asking people to fill in a form for example, then a short notice explaining why you want the information and what you will do with it will be better than having a large all-encompassing statement that is referenced on your website home page.

Bear in mind when and how you collect data. If you collect data through an App on a phone, then it is unreasonable to expect people to go onto a website to read a policy statement when they are simply using their phone.

As well as the precise wording in the Regulation, there is guidance that the UK ICO provides and we havce found that this is more readable than the Regulation. It is worth looking at the ICO website (www.ico.org.uk) to keep abreast of the advice that is published there on a regular basis as the regulation evolves as cases cause the advice to evolve.

Collect and use personal information fairly and transparently

The first principle of data protection is that personal data must be processed fairly and lawfully. You must explain who the data controller is and the purpose or purposes for which the information will be processed. This applies whether the personal data was obtained directly from the data subjects or not.

Providing a clear and concise privacy notice is an important part of fair processing. You can't be fair if you are not being honest and open about who you are and what you are going to do with the personal data you collect. However, this is only one element of fairness. Providing a privacy notice does not by itself mean that your processing is necessarily fair. You also need to consider the effect of your processing on the individuals concerned. The privacy notice that Cambridge Analytica published was fairly clear but most of the people who had their data processed didn't know that they were clients of the organization. Therefore, an important aspect of fairness includes using information in a way that people would reasonably expect.

To do this you will need to understand people's reasonable expectations about how you will use their data. Think about the impact of your processing. Will it have an adverse effect on them? Be transparent and ensure that people know how their information will be used. This means that providing your privacy notices or making them available will involve using the most appropriate mechanisms. In a digital context this can include all the on-line platforms used to deliver services.

In summary you should think about:

- what information you are collecting
- who will be collecting it
- how it will be collected.
- why you are collecting it.
- how you will use it
- if you will share it with another organization.
- if you expect the data subjects to complain.

You must also to consider the ways in which data is collected and the fact that these are changing and will continue to change. Traditionally, data was obtained directly from individuals, for example when they filled in a form on your website. Increasingly, organizations use data that has not been consciously provided by individuals in this way. It may be:

- **observed**, by tracking people on-line or by using a smart device;
- **derived** from combining other data-sets, as in a Big Data application; or
- **inferred** by using algorithms to analyse a variety of data, such as social media, location data and records of purchases in order to profile people for example in terms of their credit risk, state of health or suitability for a job. Be clear that if you are doing this, you should expect people to complain. If people object to your processing, how will you deal with this?

Give people control and choice (if they have one)

If you have relied on consent as your legal basis for processing their information you need to tell them what they are being asked to agree to and why. This should be included in your providing them with a privacy notice.

Make sure that if people have a choice, that you tell them. Consent should be freely given, specific and fully informed. It must also be revocable (i.e. people must be able to withdraw their consent) and you should have procedures in place to allow and record this.

There are times when consent is not needed, for example if someone is required by law to provide their personal details then it is wrong to suggest that they have a choice. Likewise, in an employee/employer situation you may well require the employee to provide you with their personal details. In this case it would be wrong to suggest that there is a choice.

In all of these cases it is still important to be fair and transparent. Ensuring you have effective privacy notices can help you to achieve this.

Where should you deliver privacy information to individuals?

You should not necessarily restrict your privacy notice to a single document or page on your website. The term "privacy notice" is often used as a shorthand term, but rather than seeing the task as delivering a single notice it is better to think of it as providing privacy information in a range of ways. All of the information you are giving people about how you are processing their data, taken together, constitutes the privacy information.

Communicating privacy information

You can provide privacy notices through a variety of media:

- orally – face to face or when you speak to someone on the telephone (it's a good idea to document this);
- in writing – printed media; printed adverts; forms, such as financial applications or job application forms;
- through signage – for example an information poster in a public area;
- electronically – in text messages; on websites; in emails; in mobile apps.

It is good practice to provide your privacy notices using the same method that you used to collect the data. So, if you are collecting information through an on-line form you should provide a "just-in-time notice" as the form is filled in. It would be bad practice to collect information through a form and then email the individual with a separate link to a privacy notice.

Example

Good practice is where you enter your email address and see a message explaining that it will be used for customer service purposes.

Bad practice would be to collect the data then provide a link to a separate notice elsewhere.

There are times when it is very difficult and probably not appropriate to communicate a privacy notice. For example, in an emergency situation obtaining personal details quickly can be critical to protecting an individual. In cases like these, you should explain how you use the information at an appropriate point later on, or if you can't provide privacy information, it is particularly important to make sure you only use the information you collect in a way that members of the public are likely to anticipate and agree to. Most commercial applications will not be faced with this type of decision; however, it is important to recognize that these situations can and do arise.

Use all of the technologies available when providing privacy notices. It may be valuable to consider these solutions after you have completed a DPIA. Examples of technological solutions include just-in-time, video, the functionality of devices and privacy dashboards. These can be seen as privacy-enhancing technologies because they help to protect privacy and safeguard personal data. A blended approach, incorporating a variety of these techniques is likely to be most effective. Keep the data subject as the focus when making decisions about the way to deliver privacy notices.

Layered approach

A layered approach can be useful as it allows you to provide the key privacy information immediately and have more detailed information available elsewhere for those who want it. This is used where there is not enough space to provide more detail or if you need to explain a particularly complicated information system to people.

It usually consists of a short notice containing the key information, such as the identity of the organization and the way you will use the personal information. It may contain links that expand each section to its full version, or a single link to a second, longer notice which provides more detailed information. This can, in turn, contain links to further material that explains specific issues, such as the circumstances in which information may be disclosed to the police.

How should you write a privacy notice?

One of the biggest challenges is to encourage people to read privacy information. People are often unwilling to engage with detailed explanations, particularly where they are embedded in lengthy terms and conditions. This does not mean that privacy notices are merely a formality; it means that they have to be written and presented effectively. You should:

- use clear, straightforward language;
- adopt a simple style that your audience will find easy to understand;
- not assume that everybody has the same level of understanding as you;
- avoid confusing terminology or legalistic language;
- draw on research about features of effective privacy notices when developing your own;

- align to your house style. Use expertise, for example in-house copywriters can help it fit with the style and approach your customers expect;
- align with your organization's values and principles. Doing so means that people will be more inclined to read privacy notices, understand them and trust your handling of their information;
- be truthful. Don't offer people choices that are counter-intuitive or misleading;
- follow any specific sectoral rules as well as complying with data protection law, for example in advertising or financial services sectors; and
- ensure your privacy notices are consistent across multiple platforms and enable rapid updates to them all when needed. Privacy notices can be managed using content management systems (CMS).

If you are making a major change to the way that you are wording your privacy notices, or if you are including more application data in the notices than was originally intended, then it is a good idea to roll out the updated notices early in your project process and get feedback from your customers to ensure that you are communicating effectively.

Carrying out user testing will provide useful feedback on a draft privacy notice. This is where you select a sample of your customers and ask them to use your privacy notice to obtain their feedback on:

- how they used it;
- if they found it easy to understand;
- whether anything was difficult, unclear or they did not like it; or
- if they identified any errors.

Asking your customers to do this will help you improve the effectiveness of your privacy notice. You are likely to come up with a far more useful and engaging product if you consider feedback from the people it is aimed at.

Example

You have produced a privacy notice that was based on assumptions you had made about a user's journey around your website. However, during the testing phase you identify that people are able to go to a specific page straight from a third-party search engine or can paste a URL and therefore miss some of the privacy information that you have supplied on your homepage. Having identified this, you can ensure that your privacy information is correctly connected together so that your users do not miss anything important. For example, you may provide a link to your full privacy notice in all your just-in-time notices so that an individual can then see your notice.

Post-implementation review

It is good practice to regularly review your privacy notice so that you can:

- ensure that it remains accurate and up-to-date;
- analyse complaints from the public about how you use their information and in particular any complaints about how you explain your use of their information;
- check that your privacy notice actually explains what you do with individuals' personal data; and update your privacy notice to reflect any new or amended processing.

As well as regular reviews, you should examine your privacy notice(s) whenever you change or update a process. This follows the concept of privacy by design and by default. You should incorporate this approach into your processes and check whether or not your changes impact upon the privacy information you provide. If you are relying on consent for your processing, you may also need to ask data subjects for their consent as well.

Your privacy notice checklist:

What
Confirm what to include by looking at:

- what personal information you hold;
- what you do with it and what you are planning to do with it;
- what you actually need;
- whether you are collecting the information you need;
- how long you will keep it;
- who else will have access to it;
- whether you are creating new personal information; and
- whether there are multiple data controllers.

You should also:

- display it clearly;
- ask individuals to positively opt-in;
- give them sufficient information to make a choice if they have one;
- explain the different ways you will use their information,
- state the purpose;
- provide a clear and simple way for them to indicate they agree to different types of processing;
- include a separate unticked opt-in box for direct marketing.

Think about including:

- the links between different types of data you collect and the purposes that you use each type of data for;
- the consequences of not providing information if the user has a choice;
- what you are doing to secure their personal information;
- an explanation of their right of access to their data;
- what you will not do with their data.

Where

Give privacy information:

- orally;
- in writing;
- through signage; and
- electronically.

Consider a layered approach:

- just-in-time notices;
- video;
- icons and symbols; and
- privacy dashboards.

When

Actively give privacy information if:

- you are collecting sensitive information;
- the intended use of the information is likely to be unexpected or objectionable;
- providing personal information, or failing to do so, will have a significant effect on the individual; or
- the information will be shared with another organization in a way that individuals would not expect.

How

Write and present it effectively:

- Use clear, straightforward language.
- Adopt a style that your audience will understand.
- Don't assume that everybody has the same level of understanding as you; avoid confusing terminology or legalistic language.

- Draw on research about features of effective privacy notices.
- Align to your house style.
- Align with your organization's values and principles.
- Be truthful. Don't offer people choices that are counter-intuitive or misleading.
- Follow any specific sectoral rules.
- Ensure all your notices are consistent and can be updated rapidly; and
- Provide separate notices for different audiences.

Test and review

Before roll out:

- Test your draft privacy notice with users;
- Amend it if necessary.

After roll out:

- Keep your privacy notice under review.
- Take account of any complaints about information handling.
- Update it as necessary to reflect any changes in your collection and use of personal data.

While the above advice was written for the UK, it is a good check-list and we suggest that you may want to follow it.

For consent you must record and track the consent. You should maintain an audit trail of who gave their consent, when and how (was it by email or ticking a box). If you retain the fact that you have their permission, then if the customer later forgets and claims that you do not have their permission, you can demonstrate that you have acted in good faith. This also applies if you wish to sell a list of your customers. You must ensure that they have agreed to you passing on their details.

If you buy in marketing lists, then you will need to ensure that the supplier has confirmed that their customers have opted in to marketing and that they have agreed that their data could be sold. You will also need to check if any of the people on the new list have previously opted out of marketing and remove these people from your list.

Section

14

The Regulation

The complete Regulation runs to 99 Articles with 173 Recitals that clarify what the Regulation means. The Acts will remain static for some time but the Recitals are likely to be expanded as the EU and the Courts deal with test cases over time. It is worth downloading the complete Regulation and reviewing it from time to time to make sure you have the latest version. However, we have included the most relevant Acts here, along with the Recitals that relate to them so you have them as a handy reference point.

The EU General Data Protection Regulation

CHAPTER I GENERAL PROVISIONS

Article 1 Subject Matter and Objectives

1. This Regulation lays down rules relating to the protection of natural persons with regard to the processing of personal data and rules relating to the free movement of personal data.
2. This Regulation protects fundamental rights and freedoms of natural persons and in particular their right to the protection of personal data.
3. The free movement of personal data within the Union shall be neither restricted nor prohibited for reasons connected with the protection of natural persons with regard to the processing of personal data.

Relevant Recitals

(1) Data protection as a fundamental right
(2) Respect of the fundamental rights and freedoms

(3) Directive 95/46/EC harmonisation
(4) Data protection in balance with other fundamental rights
(5) Cooperation between Member States to exchange personal data
(6) Ensuring a high level of data protection despite the increased exchange of data
(7) The framework is based on control and certainty
(8) Adoption into national law
(9) Different standards of protection by the Directive 95/45/EC
(10) Harmonised level of data protection despite national scope
(11) Harmonisation of the powers and sanctions
(12) Authorisation of the European Parliament and the Council

Article 2 Material Scope

1. This Regulation applies to the processing of personal data wholly or partly by automated means and to the processing other than by automated means of personal data which form part of a filing system or are intended to form part of a filing system.
2. This Regulation does not apply to the processing of personal data:

    a) in the course of an activity which falls outside the scope of Union law;
    b) by the Member States when carrying out activities which fall within the scope of Chapter II of Title V of the TEU;
    c) by a natural person in the course of a purely personal or household activity;
    d) by competent authorities for the purposes of the prevention, investigation, detection or prosecution of criminal offences or the execution of criminal penalties, including the safeguarding against and the prevention of threats to public security.

3. For the processing of personal data by the Union institutions, bodies, offices and agencies, Regulation (EC) No 45/2001 applies. Regulation (EC) No 45/2001 and other Union legal acts applicable to such processing of personal data shall be adapted to the principles and rules of this Regulation in accordance with Article 98.
4. This Regulation shall be without prejudice to the application of Directive 2000/31/EC, in particular of the liability rules of intermediary service providers in Articles 12 to 15 of that Directive.

Relevant Recitals

(13) Taking account of micro, small and medium-sized enterprises
(14) Not applicable to legal persons
(15) Technology neutrality

(16) Not applicable to activities regarding national and common security

(17) Adaptation of Regulation (EC) No 45/2001

(18) Not applicable to personal or household activities

(19) Not applicable to criminal prosecution

(20) Respecting the independence of the judiciary

(21) Liability rules of intermediary service providers shall remain unaffected

(27) Not applicable to data of deceased persons

Article 3 Territorial Scope

1. This Regulation applies to the processing of personal data in the context of the activities of an establishment of a controller or a processor in the Union, regardless of whether the processing takes place in the Union or not.

2. This Regulation applies to the processing of personal data of data subjects who are in the Union by a controller or processor not established in the Union, where the processing activities are related to:

   a) the offering of goods or services, irrespective of whether a payment of the data subject is required, to such data subjects in the Union; or

   b) the monitoring of their behaviour as far as their behaviour takes place within the Union.

3. This Regulation applies to the processing of personal data by a controller not established in the Union, but in a place where Member State law applies by virtue of public international law.

Relevant Recitals

(22) Processing by an establishment

(23) Applicable to processors not established in the Union if data subjects within the Union are targeted

(24) Applicable to processors not established in the Union if data subjects within the Union are profiled

(25) Applicable to processors due to international law

Article 4 Definitions

For the purposes of this Regulation:

1. 'personal data' means any information relating to an identified or identifiable natural person ('data subject'); an identifiable natural person is one who can be identified, directly or indirectly, in particular by reference to an identifier such

as a name, an identification number, location data, an online identifier or to one or more factors specific to the physical, physiological, genetic, mental, economic, cultural or social identity of that natural person;

2. 'processing' means any operation or set of operations which is performed on personal data or on sets of personal data, whether or not by automated means, such as collection, recording, organisation, structuring, storage, adaptation or alteration, retrieval, consultation, use, disclosure by transmission, dissemination or otherwise making available, alignment or combination, restriction, erasure or destruction;

3. 'restriction of processing' means the marking of stored personal data with the aim of limiting their processing in the future;

4. 'profiling' means any form of automated processing of personal data consisting of the use of personal data to evaluate certain personal aspects relating to a natural person, in particular to analyse or predict aspects concerning that natural person's performance at work, economic situation, health, personal preferences, interests, reliability, behaviour, location or movements;

5. 'pseudonymisation' means the processing of personal data in such a manner that the personal data can no longer be attributed to a specific data subject without the use of additional information, provided that such additional information is kept separately and is subject to technical and organisational measures to ensure that the personal data are not attributed to an identified or identifiable natural person;

6. 'filing system' means any structured set of personal data which are accessible according to specific criteria, whether centralised, decentralised or dispersed on a functional or geographical basis;

7. 'controller' means the natural or legal person, public authority, agency or other body which, alone or jointly with others, determines the purposes and means of the processing of personal data; where the purposes and means of such processing are determined by Union or Member State law, the controller or the specific criteria for its nomination may be provided for by Union or Member State law;

8. 'processor' means a natural or legal person, public authority, agency or other body which processes personal data on behalf of the controller;

9. 'recipient' means a natural or legal person, public authority, agency or another body, to which the personal data are disclosed, whether a third party or not. However, public authorities which may receive personal data in the framework of a particular inquiry in accordance with Union or Member State law shall not be regarded as recipients; the processing of those data by those public authorities shall be in compliance with the applicable data protection rules according to the purposes of the processing;

10. 'third party' means a natural or legal person, public authority, agency or body other than the data subject, controller, processor and persons who, under the direct authority of the controller or processor, are authorised to process personal data;

11. 'consent' of the data subject means any freely given, specific, informed and unambiguous indication of the data subject's wishes by which he or she, by a

statement or by a clear affirmative action, signifies agreement to the processing of personal data relating to him or her;

12. 'personal data breach' means a breach of security leading to the accidental or unlawful destruction, loss, alteration, unauthorised disclosure of, or access to, personal data transmitted, stored or otherwise processed;

13. 'genetic data' means personal data relating to the inherited or acquired genetic characteristics of a natural person which give unique information about the physiology or the health of that natural person and which result, in particular, from an analysis of a biological sample from the natural person in question;

14. 'biometric data' means personal data resulting from specific technical processing relating to the physical, physiological or behavioural characteristics of a natural person, which allow or confirm the unique identification of that natural person, such as facial images or dactyloscopic data;

15. 'data concerning health' means personal data related to the physical or mental health of a natural person, including the provision of health care services, which reveal information about his or her health status;

16. 'main establishment' means:

   a) as regards a controller with establishments in more than one Member State, the place of its central administration in the Union, unless the decisions on the purposes and means of the processing of personal data are taken in another establishment of the controller in the Union and the latter establishment has the power to have such decisions implemented, in which case the establishment having taken such decisions is to be considered to be the main establishment;

   b) as regards a processor with establishments in more than one Member State, the place of its central administration in the Union, or, if the processor has no central administration in the Union, the establishment of the processor in the Union where the main processing activities in the context of the activities of an establishment of the processor take place to the extent that the processor is subject to specific obligations under this Regulation;

17. 'representative' means a natural or legal person established in the Union who, designated by the controller or processor in writing pursuant to Article 27, represents the controller or processor with regard to their respective obligations under this Regulation;

18. 'enterprise' means a natural or legal person engaged in an economic activity, irrespective of its legal form, including partnerships or associations regularly engaged in an economic activity;

19. 'group of undertakings' means a controlling undertaking and its controlled undertakings;

20. 'binding corporate rules' means personal data protection policies which are adhered to by a controller or processor established on the territory of a Member State for transfers or a set of transfers of personal data to a controller

or processor in one or more third countries within a group of undertakings, or group of enterprises engaged in a joint economic activity;

21. 'supervisory authority' means an independent public authority which is established by a Member State pursuant to Article 51;

22. 'supervisory authority concerned' means a supervisory authority which is concerned by the processing of personal data because:

    a) the controller or processor is established on the territory of the Member State of that supervisory authority;
    b) data subjects residing in the Member State of that supervisory authority are substantially affected or likely to be substantially affected by the processing; or
    c) a complaint has been lodged with that supervisory authority;

23. 'cross–border processing' means either:

    a) processing of personal data which takes place in the context of the activities of establishments in more than one Member State of a controller or processor in the Union where the controller or processor is established in more than one Member State; or
    b) processing of personal data which takes place in the context of the activities of a single establishment of a controller or processor in the Union but which substantially affects or is likely to substantially affect data subjects in more than one Member State.

24. 'relevant and reasoned objection' means an objection to a draft decision as to whether there is an infringement of this Regulation, or whether envisaged action in relation to the controller or processor complies with this Regulation, which clearly demonstrates the significance of the risks posed by the draft decision as regards the fundamental rights and freedoms of data subjects and, where applicable, the free flow of personal data within the Union;

25. 'information society service' means a service as defined in point (b) of Article 1(1) of Directive (EU) 2015/1535 of the European Parliament and of the Council (');

26. 'international organisation' means an organisation and its subordinate bodies governed by public international law, or any other body which is set up by, or on the basis of, an agreement between two or more countries.

Relevant Recitals

(15) Technology neutrality

(24) Applicable to processors not established in the Union if data subjects within the Union are profiled

(26) Not applicable to anonymous data

(28) Introduction of pseudonymisation

(29) Pseudonymisation at the same controller
(30) Online identifiers for profiling and identification
(31) Not applicable to public authorities in connection with their official tasks
(34) Genetic data
(35) Health data
(36) Determination of the main establishment
(37) Enterprise group

CHAPTER II PRINCIPLES

Article 5 Principles relating to processing of Personal Information

1. Personal data shall be:

   a) processed lawfully, fairly and in a transparent manner in relation to the data subject ('lawfulness, fairness and transparency');

   b) collected for specified, explicit and legitimate purposes and not further processed in a manner that is incompatible with those purposes; further processing for archiving purposes in the public interest, scientific or historical research purposes or statistical purposes shall, in accordance with Article 89(1), not be considered to be incompatible with the initial purposes ('purpose limitation');

   c) adequate, relevant and limited to what is necessary in relation to the purposes for which they are processed ('data minimisation');

   d) accurate and, where necessary, kept up to date; every reasonable step must be taken to ensure that personal data that are inaccurate, having regard to the purposes for which they are processed, are erased or rectified without delay ('accuracy');

   e) kept in a form which permits identification of data subjects for no longer than is necessary for the purposes for which the personal data are processed; personal data may be stored for longer periods insofar as the personal data will be processed solely for archiving purposes in the public interest, scientific or historical research purposes or statistical purposes in accordance with Article 89(1) subject to implementation of the appropriate technical and organisational measures required by this Regulation in order to safeguard the rights and freedoms of the data subject ('storage limitation');

   f) processed in a manner that ensures appropriate security of the personal data, including protection against unauthorised or unlawful processing and against accidental loss, destruction or damage, using appropriate technical or organisational measures ('integrity and confidentiality').

2. The controller shall be responsible for, and be able to demonstrate compliance with, paragraph 1 ('accountability').

Relevant Recital

(39) Principles relating to data processing

Article 6 Lawfulness of Processing

1. Processing shall be lawful only if and to the extent that at least one of the following applies:

   a) the data subject has given consent to the processing of his or her personal data for one or more specific purposes;

   b) processing is necessary for the performance of a contract to which the data subject is party or in order to take steps at the request of the data subject prior to entering into a contract;

   c) processing is necessary for compliance with a legal obligation to which the controller is subject;

   d) processing is necessary in order to protect the vital interests of the data subject or of another natural person;

   e) processing is necessary for the performance of a task carried out in the public interest or in the exercise of official authority vested in the controller;

   f) processing is necessary for the purposes of the legitimate interests pursued by the controller or by a third party, except where such interests are overridden by the interests or fundamental rights and freedoms of the data subject which require protection of personal data, in particular where the data subject is a child.

   Point (f) of the first subparagraph shall not apply to processing carried out by public authorities in the performance of their tasks.

2. Member States may maintain or introduce more specific provisions to adapt the application of the rules of this Regulation with regard to processing for compliance with points (c) and (e) of paragraph 1 by determining more precisely specific requirements for the processing and other measures to ensure lawful and fair processing including for other specific processing situations as provided for in Chapter IX.

3. The basis for the processing referred to in point (c) and (e) of paragraph 1 shall be laid down by:

   a) Union law; or

   b) Member State law to which the controller is subject.

The purpose of the processing shall be determined in that legal basis or, as regards the processing referred to in point (e) of paragraph 1, shall be necessary for the performance of a task carried out in the public interest or in the exercise of official authority vested in the controller. That legal basis may contain specific provisions to adapt the application of rules of this Regulation, inter alia: the general conditions governing the lawfulness of processing by the controller; the types of data which are subject to the processing; the data subjects concerned; the entities to, and the purposes for which, the personal data may be disclosed; the purpose limitation; storage periods; and processing operations and processing procedures, including measures to ensure lawful and fair processing such as those for other specific processing situations as provided for in Chapter IX. The Union or the Member State law shall meet an objective of public interest and be proportionate to the legitimate aim pursued.

4. Where the processing for a purpose other than that for which the personal data have been collected is not based on the data subject's consent or on a Union or Member State law which constitutes a necessary and proportionate measure in a democratic society to safeguard the objectives referred to in Article 23(1), the controller shall, in order to ascertain whether processing for another purpose is compatible with the purpose for which the personal data are initially collected, take into account, inter alia:

    a) any link between the purposes for which the personal data have been collected and the purposes of the intended further processing;
    b) the context in which the personal data have been collected, in particular regarding the relationship between data subjects and the controller;
    c) the nature of the personal data, in particular whether special categories of personal data are processed, pursuant to Article 9, or whether personal data related to criminal convictions and offences are processed, pursuant to Article 10;
    d) the possible consequences of the intended further processing for data subjects;
    e) the existence of appropriate safeguards, which may include encryption or pseudonymisation.

Relevant Recitals

(39) Principles relating to data processing
(40) Lawfulness relating to data processing
(41) Legal basis and/or legislative measures
(42) Burden of proof and requirements for consent
(43) Freely given consent
(44) Performance of a contract
(45) Fulfilment of legal obligations
(46) Vital interests of the data subject
(47) Overriding legitimate interest

(48) Overriding legitimate interest within group of undertakings
(49) Network and information security as overriding legitimate interest
(50) Further processing of personal data
(171) Repeal of Directive 95/46/EC and transitional provisions

Article 7 Conditions for Consent

1. Where processing is based on consent, the controller shall be able to demonstrate that the data subject has consented to processing of his or her personal data.

2. If the data subject's consent is given in the context of a written declaration which also concerns other matters, the request for consent shall be presented in a manner which is clearly distinguishable from the other matters, in an intelligible and easily accessible form, using clear and plain language. Any part of such a declaration which constitutes an infringement of this Regulation shall not be binding.

3. The data subject shall have the right to withdraw his or her consent at any time. The withdrawal of consent shall not affect the lawfulness of processing based on consent before its withdrawal. Prior to giving consent, the data subject shall be informed thereof. It shall be as easy to withdraw as to give consent.

4. When assessing whether consent is freely given, utmost account shall be taken of whether, *inter alia*, the performance of a contract, including the provision of a service, is conditional on consent to the processing of personal data that is not necessary for the performance of that contract.

Relevant Recitals

(32) Conditions relating to and for consent
(33) Consent to certain areas of scientific research
(42) Burden of proof and requirements for consent
(43) Freely given consent

Article 8 Conditions applicable to child's consent in relation to information society services

1. Where point (a) of Article 6(1) applies, in relation to the offer of information society services directly to a child, the processing of the personal data of a child shall be lawful where the child is at least 16 years old. Where the child is below the age of 16 years, such processing shall be lawful only if and to the extent that consent is given or authorised by the holder of parental responsibility over the child.Member States may provide by law for a lower age for those purposes provided that such lower age is not below 13 years.

2. The controller shall make reasonable efforts to verify in such cases that consent is given or authorised by the holder of parental responsibility over the child, taking into consideration available technology.
3. Paragraph 1 shall not affect the general contract law of Member States such as the rules on the validity, formation or effect of a contract in relation to a child.

Relevant Recital

(38) Special protection of children's personal data

Article 9 Processing of special categories of personal data

1. Processing of personal data revealing racial or ethnic origin, political opinions, religious or philosophical beliefs, or trade union membership, and the processing of genetic data, biometric data for the purpose of uniquely identifying a natural person, data concerning health or data concerning a natural person's sex life or sexual orientation shall be prohibited.
2. Paragraph 1 shall not apply if one of the following applies:

   a) the data subject has given explicit consent to the processing of those personal data for one or more specified purposes, except where Union or Member State law provide that the prohibition referred to in paragraph 1 may not be lifted by the data subject;

   b) processing is necessary for the purposes of carrying out the obligations and exercising specific rights of the controller or of the data subject in the field of employment and social security and social protection law in so far as it is authorised by Union or Member State law or a collective agreement pursuant to Member State law providing for appropriate safeguards for the fundamental rights and the interests of the data subject;

   c) processing is necessary to protect the vital interests of the data subject or of another natural person where the data subject is physically or legally incapable of giving consent;

   d) processing is carried out in the course of its legitimate activities with appropriate safeguards by a foundation, association or any other not-for-profit body with a political, philosophical, religious or trade union aim and on condition that the processing relates solely to the members or to former members of the body or to persons who have regular contact with it in connection with its purposes and that the personal data are not disclosed outside that body without the consent of the data subjects;

   e) processing relates to personal data which are manifestly made public by the data subject;

   f)   processing is necessary for the establishment, exercise or defence of legal claims or whenever courts are acting in their judicial capacity;

   g)   processing is necessary for reasons of substantial public interest, on the basis of Union or Member State law which shall be proportionate to the aim pursued, respect the essence of the right to data protection and provide for suitable and specific measures to safeguard the fundamental rights and the interests of the data subject;

   h)   processing is necessary for the purposes of preventive or occupational medicine, for the assessment of the working capacity of the employee, medical diagnosis, the provision of health or social care or treatment or the management of health or social care systems and services on the basis of Union or Member State law or pursuant to contract with a health professional and subject to the conditions and safeguards referred to in paragraph 3;

   i)   processing is necessary for reasons of public interest in the area of public health, such as protecting against serious cross-border threats to health or ensuring high standards of quality and safety of health care and of medicinal products or medical devices, on the basis of Union or Member State law which provides for suitable and specific measures to safeguard the rights and freedoms of the data subject, in particular professional secrecy;

   j)   processing is necessary for archiving purposes in the public interest, scientific or historical research purposes or statistical purposes in accordance with Article 89(1) based on Union or Member State law which shall be proportionate to the aim pursued, respect the essence of the right to data protection and provide for suitable and specific measures to safeguard the fundamental rights and the interests of the data subject.

3.   Personal data referred to in paragraph 1 may be processed for the purposes referred to in point (h) of paragraph 2 when those data are processed by or under the responsibility of a professional subject to the obligation of professional secrecy under Union or Member State law or rules established by national competent bodies or by another person also subject to an obligation of secrecy under Union or Member State law or rules established by national competent bodies.

4.   Member States may maintain or introduce further conditions, including limitations, with regard to the processing of genetic data, biometric data or data concerning health.

Relevant Recitals

(46) Vital interests of the data subject

(51) Protecting sensitive personal data

(52) Exceptions to the prohibition on processing special categories of personal data
(53) Processing of sensitive data in health and social sector
(54) Processing of sensitive data in public health sector
(55) Public interest in processing by official authorities for objectives of recognized religious communities
(56) Processing personal data on people's political opinions by parties

Article 10 Processing of personal data relating to criminal convictions and offences

Processing of personal data relating to criminal convictions and offences or related security measures based on Article 6(1) shall be carried out only under the control of official authority or when the processing is authorised by Union or Member State law providing for appropriate safeguards for the rights and freedoms of data subjects. Any comprehensive register of criminal convictions shall be kept only under the control of official authority.

Relevant Recitals

(50) Further processing of personal data

Article 11 Processing which does not require identification

1. If the purposes for which a controller processes personal data do not or do no longer require the identification of a data subject by the controller, the controller shall not be obliged to maintain, acquire or process additional information in order to identify the data subject for the sole purpose of complying with this Regulation.
2. Where, in cases referred to in paragraph 1 of this Article, the controller is able to demonstrate that it is not in a position to identify the data subject, the controller shall inform the data subject accordingly, if possible. In such cases, Articles 15 to 20 shall not apply except where the data subject, for the purpose of exercising his or her rights under those articles, provides additional information enabling his or her identification.

Relevant Recital

(57) Additional data for identification purposes

CHAPTER III RIGHTS OF THE DATA SUBJECT

Article 12 Transparent information, communication and modalities for the exercise of the rights of the data subject

1. The controller shall take appropriate measures to provide any information referred to in Articles 13 and 14 and any communication under Articles 15 to 22 and 34 relating to processing to the data subject in a concise, transparent, intelligible and easily accessible form, using clear and plain language, in particular for any information addressed specifically to a child. The information shall be provided in writing, or by other means, including, where appropriate, by electronic means. When requested by the data subject, the information may be provided orally, provided that the identity of the data subject is proven by other means.

2. The controller shall facilitate the exercise of data subject rights under Articles 15 to 22. In the cases referred to in Article 11(2), the controller shall not refuse to act on the request of the data subject for exercising his or her rights under Articles 15 to 22, unless the controller demonstrates that it is not in a position to identify the data subject.

3. The controller shall provide information on action taken on a request under Articles 15 to 22 to the data subject without undue delay and in any event within one month of receipt of the request. That period may be extended by two further months where necessary, taking into account the complexity and number of the requests. The controller shall inform the data subject of any such extension within one month of receipt of the request, together with the reasons for the delay. Where the data subject makes the request by electronic form means, the information shall be provided by electronic means where possible, unless otherwise requested by the data subject.

4. If the controller does not take action on the request of the data subject, the controller shall inform the data subject without delay and at the latest within one month of receipt of the request of the reasons for not taking action and on the possibility of lodging a complaint with a supervisory authority and seeking a judicial remedy.

5. Information provided under Articles 13 and 14 and any communication and any actions taken under Articles 15 to 22 and 34 shall be provided free of charge. Where requests from a data subject are manifestly unfounded or excessive, in particular because of their repetitive character, the controller may either:

   a) charge a reasonable fee taking into account the administrative costs of providing the information or communication or taking the action requested; or

   b) refuse to act on the request.

The controller shall bear the burden of demonstrating the manifestly unfounded or excessive character of the request.

6. Without prejudice to Article 11, where the controller has reasonable doubts concerning the identity of the natural person making the request referred to in Articles 15 to 21, the controller may request the provision of additional information necessary to confirm the identity of the data subject.

7. The information to be provided to data subjects pursuant to Articles 13 and 14 may be provided in combination with standardised icons in order to give in an easily visible, intelligible and clearly legible manner a meaningful overview of the intended processing. Where the icons are presented electronically they shall be machine-readable.

8. The Commission shall be empowered to adopt delegated acts in accordance with Article 92 for the purpose of determining the information to be presented by the icons and the procedures for providing standardised icons.

Relevant Recitals

(58) The principle of transparency
(59) Procedures relating to the exercise of the rights of the data subjects
(60) Information obligation
(73) Restrictions of rights and principles

Article 13 Information to be provided where personal data are collected from the data subject

1. Where personal data relating to a data subject are collected from the data subject, the controller shall, at the time when personal data are obtained, provide the data subject with all of the following information:

   a) the identity and the contact details of the controller and, where applicable, of the controller's representative;

   b) the contact details of the data protection officer, where applicable;

   c) the purposes of the processing for which the personal data are intended as well as the legal basis for the processing;

   d) where the processing is based on point (f) of Article 6(1), the legitimate interests pursued by the controller or by a third party;

   e) the recipients or categories of recipients of the personal data, if any;

   f) where applicable, the fact that the controller intends to transfer personal data to a third country or international organisation and the existence or absence of an adequacy decision by the Commission, or in the case of transfers referred to in Article 46 or 47, or the second subparagraph of Article 49(1), reference to the appropriate or suitable safeguards and the means by which to obtain a copy of them or where they have been made available.

2.   In addition to the information referred to in paragraph 1, the controller shall, at the time when personal data are obtained, provide the data subject with the following further information necessary to ensure fair and transparent processing:

a)   the period for which the personal data will be stored, or if that is not possible, the criteria used to determine that period;

b)   the existence of the right to request from the controller access to and rectification or erasure of personal data or restriction of processing concerning the data subject or to object to processing as well as the right to data portability;

c)   where the processing is based on point (a) of Article 6(1) or point (a) of Article 9(2), the existence of the right to withdraw consent at any time, without affecting the lawfulness of processing based on consent before its withdrawal;

d)   the right to lodge a complaint with a supervisory authority;

e)   whether the provision of personal data is a statutory or contractual requirement, or a requirement necessary to enter into a contract, as well as whether the data subject is obliged to provide the personal data and of the possible consequences of failure to provide such data;

f)   the existence of automated decision-making, including profiling, referred to in Article 22(1) and (4) and, at least in those cases, meaningful information about the logic involved, as well as the significance and the envisaged consequences of such processing for the data subject.

3.   Where the controller intends to further process the personal data for a purpose other than that for which the personal data were collected, the controller shall provide the data subject prior to that further processing with information on that other purpose and with any relevant further information as referred to in paragraph 2.

4.   Paragraphs 1, 2 and 3 shall not apply where and insofar as the data subject already has the information.

Relevant Recitals

(60) Information obligation
(61) Time of information
(62) Exceptions to the obligation to provide information

Article 14 Information to be provided where personal data have not been obtained from the data subject

1.   Where personal data have not been obtained from the data subject, the controller shall provide the data subject with the following information:

a) the identity and the contact details of the controller and, where applicable, of the controller's representative;

b) the contact details of the data protection officer, where applicable;

c) the purposes of the processing for which the personal data are intended as well as the legal basis for the processing;

d) the categories of personal data concerned;

e) the recipients or categories of recipients of the personal data, if any;

f) where applicable, that the controller intends to transfer personal data to a recipient in a third country or international organisation and the existence or absence of an adequacy decision by the Commission, or in the case of transfers referred to in Article 46 or 47, or the second subparagraph of Article 49(1), reference to the appropriate or suitable safeguards and the means to obtain a copy of them or where they have been made available.

2. In addition to the information referred to in paragraph 1, the controller shall provide the data subject with the following information necessary to ensure fair and transparent processing in respect of the data subject:

a) the period for which the personal data will be stored, or if that is not possible, the criteria used to determine that period;

b) where the processing is based on point (f) of Article 6(1), the legitimate interests pursued by the controller or by a third party;

c) the existence of the right to request from the controller access to and rectification or erasure of personal data or restriction of processing concerning the data subject and to object to processing as well as the right to data portability;

d) where processing is based on point (a) of Article 6(1) or point (a) of Article 9(2), the existence of the right to withdraw consent at any time, without affecting the lawfulness of processing based on consent before its withdrawal;

e) the right to lodge a complaint with a supervisory authority;

f) from which source the personal data originate, and if applicable, whether it came from publicly accessible sources;

g) the existence of automated decision–making, including profiling, referred to in Article 22(1) and (4) and, at least in those cases, meaningful information about the logic involved, as well as the significance and the envisaged consequences of such processing for the data subject.

3. The controller shall provide the information referred to in paragraphs 1 and 2:

a) within a reasonable period after obtaining the personal data, but at the latest within one month, having regard to the specific circumstances in which the personal data are processed;

b) if the personal data are to be used for communication with the data subject, at the latest at the time of the first communication to that data subject; or

c) if a disclosure to another recipient is envisaged, at the latest when the personal data are first disclosed.

4. Where the controller intends to further process the personal data for a purpose other than that for which the personal data were obtained, the controller shall provide the data subject prior to that further processing with information on that other purpose and with any relevant further information as referred to in paragraph 2.

5. Paragraphs 1 to 4 shall not apply where and insofar as:

a) the data subject already has the information;

b) the provision of such information proves impossible or would involve a disproportionate effort, in particular for processing for archiving purposes in the public interest, scientific or historical research purposes or statistical purposes, subject to the conditions and safeguards referred to in Article 89 (1) or in so far as the obligation referred to in paragraph 1 of this Article is likely to render impossible or seriously impair the achievement of the objectives of that processing. In such cases the controller shall take appropriate measures to protect the data subject's rights and freedoms and legitimate interests, including making the information publicly available;

c) obtaining or disclosure is expressly laid down by Union or Member State law to which the controller is subject and which provides appropriate measures to protect the data subject's legitimate interests; or

d) where the personal data must remain confidential subject to an obligation of professional secrecy regulated by Union or Member State law, including a statutory obligation of secrecy.

Relevant Recitals

(60) Information obligation
(61) Time of information
(62) Exceptions to the obligation to provide information

Article 15 Right of access by the data subject

1. The data subject shall have the right to obtain from the controller confirmation as to whether or not personal data concerning him or her are being processed, and, where that is the case, access to the personal data and the following information:

a) the purposes of the processing;

b) the categories of personal data concerned;

c) the recipients or categories of recipient to whom the personal data have been or will be disclosed, in particular recipients in third countries or international organisations;

d) where possible, the envisaged period for which the personal data will be stored, or, if not possible, the criteria used to determine that period;

e) the existence of the right to request from the controller rectification or erasure of personal data or restriction of processing of personal data concerning the data subject or to object to such processing;

f) the right to lodge a complaint with a supervisory authority;

g) where the personal data are not collected from the data subject, any available information as to their source;

h) the existence of automated decision-making, including profiling, referred to in Article 22(1) and (4) and, at least in those cases, meaningful information about the logic involved, as well as the significance and the envisaged consequences of such processing for the data subject.

2. Where personal data are transferred to a third country or to an international organisation, the data subject shall have the right to be informed of the appropriate safeguards pursuant to Article 46 relating to the transfer.

3. The controller shall provide a copy of the personal data undergoing processing. For any further copies requested by the data subject, the controller may charge a reasonable fee based on administrative costs. Where the data subject makes the request by electronic means, and unless otherwise requested by the data subject, the information shall be provided in a commonly used electronic form.

4. The right to obtain a copy referred to in paragraph 3 shall not adversely affect the rights and freedoms of others.

Relevant Recitals

(63) Right of access
(64) Identity verification

Article 16 Right to rectification

The data subject shall have the right to obtain from the controller without undue delay the rectification of inaccurate personal data concerning him or her. Taking into account the purposes of the processing, the data subject shall have the right to have incomplete personal data completed, including by means of providing a supplementary statement.

Relevant Recital

(65) Right of rectification and erasure

Article 17 Right to erasure ('right to be forgotten')

1. The data subject shall have the right to obtain from the controller the erasure of personal data concerning him or her without undue delay and the controller shall have the obligation to erase personal data without undue delay where one of the following grounds applies:

    a) the personal data are no longer necessary in relation to the purposes for which they were collected or otherwise processed;
    b) the data subject withdraws consent on which the processing is based according to point (a) of Article 6(1), or point (a) of Article 9(2), and where there is no other legal ground for the processing;
    c) the data subject objects to the processing pursuant to Article 21(1) and there are no overriding legitimate grounds for the processing, or the data subject objects to the processing pursuant to Article 21(2);
    d) the personal data have been unlawfully processed;
    e) the personal data have to be erased for compliance with a legal obligation in Union or Member State law to which the controller is subject;
    f) the personal data have been collected in relation to the offer of information society services referred to in Article 8(1).

2. Where the controller has made the personal data public and is obliged pursuant to paragraph 1 to erase the personal data, the controller, taking account of available technology and the cost of implementation, shall take reasonable steps, including technical measures, to inform controllers who are processing the personal data that the data subject has requested the erasure by such controllers of any links to, or copy or replication of, those personal data.

3. Paragraphs 1 and 2 shall not apply to the extent that processing is necessary:

    a) for exercising the right of freedom of expression and information;
    b) for compliance with a legal obligation which requires processing by Union or Member State law to which the controller is subject or for the performance of a task carried out in the public interest or in the exercise of official authority vested in the controller;
    c) for reasons of public interest in the area of public health in accordance with points (h) and (i) of Article 9(2) as well as Article 9(3);
    d) for archiving purposes in the public interest, scientific or historical research purposes or statistical purposes in accordance with Article 89(1) in so far as the right referred to in paragraph 1 is likely to render impossible or seriously impair the achievement of the objectives of that processing; or
    e) for the establishment, exercise or defence of legal claims.

Relevant Recitals

(65) Right of rectification and erasure
(66) Right to be forgotten

Article 18 Right to restriction of processing

1. The data subject shall have the right to obtain from the controller restriction of processing where one of the following applies:

    a) the accuracy of the personal data is contested by the data subject for a period enabling the controller to verify the accuracy of the personal data;
    b) the processing is unlawful and the data subject opposes the erasure of the personal data and requests the restriction of their use instead;
    c) the controller no longer needs the personal data for the purposes of the processing, but they are required by the data subject for the establishment, exercise or defence of legal claims;
    d) the data subject has objected to processing pursuant to Article 21(1) pending the verification whether the legitimate grounds of the controller override those of the data subject.

2. Where processing has been restricted under paragraph 1, such personal data shall, with the exception of storage, only be processed with the data subject's consent or for the establishment, exercise or defence of legal claims or for the protection of the rights of another natural or legal person or for reasons of important public interest of the Union or of a Member State.

3. A data subject who has obtained restriction of processing pursuant to paragraph 1 shall be informed by the controller before the restriction of processing is lifted.

Relevant Recital

(67) Restriction of processing

Article 19 Notification obligation regarding rectification or erasure of personal data or restriction of processing

The controller shall communicate any rectification or erasure of personal data or restriction of processing carried out in accordance with Article 16, Article 17(1) and Article 18 to each recipient to whom the personal data have been disclosed, unless this proves impossible or involves disproportionate effort. The controller shall inform the data subject about those recipients if the data subject requests it.

Relevant Recital

(66) Right to be forgotten

Article 20 Right to data portability

1. The data subject shall have the right to receive the personal data concerning him or her, which he or she has provided to a controller, in a structured, commonly used and machine-readable format and have the right to transmit those data to another controller without hindrance from the controller to which the personal data have been provided, where:

    a) the processing is based on consent pursuant to point (a) of Article 6(1) or point (a) of Article 9(2) or on a contract pursuant to point (b) of Article 6(1); and
    b) the processing is carried out by automated means.

2. In exercising his or her right to data portability pursuant to paragraph 1, the data subject shall have the right to have the personal data transmitted directly from one controller to another, where technically feasible.
3. The exercise of the right referred to in paragraph 1 of this Article shall be without prejudice to Article 17. That right shall not apply to processing necessary for the performance of a task carried out in the public interest or in the exercise of official authority vested in the controller.
4. The right referred to in paragraph 1 shall not adversely affect the rights and freedoms of others.

Relevant Recital

(68) Right of data portability

Article 21 Right to Object

1. The data subject shall have the right to object, on grounds relating to his or her particular situation, at any time to processing of personal data concerning him or her which is based on point (e) or (f) of Article 6(1), including profiling based on those provisions. The controller shall no longer process the personal data unless the controller demonstrates compelling legitimate grounds for the processing which override the interests, rights and freedoms of the data subject or for the establishment, exercise or defence of legal claims.
2. Where personal data are processed for direct marketing purposes, the data subject shall have the right to object at any time to processing of personal data concerning

him or her for such marketing, which includes profiling to the extent that it is related to such direct marketing.

3.   Where the data subject objects to processing for direct marketing purposes, the personal data shall no longer be processed for such purposes.

4.   At the latest at the time of the first communication with the data subject, the right referred to in paragraphs 1 and 2 shall be explicitly brought to the attention of the data subject and shall be presented clearly and separately from any other information.

5.   In the context of the use of information society services, and notwithstanding Directive 2002/58/EC, the data subject may exercise his or her right to object by automated means using technical specifications.

6.   Where personal data are processed for scientific or historical research purposes or statistical purposes pursuant to Article 89(1), the data subject, on grounds relating to his or her particular situation, shall have the right to object to processing of personal data concerning him or her, unless the processing is necessary for the performance of a task carried out for reasons of public interest.

Relevant Recitals

(69) Right to object
(70) Right to object to direct marketing

Article 22 Automated individual decision-making, including profiling

1.   The data subject shall have the right not to be subject to a decision based solely on automated processing, including profiling, which produces legal effects concerning him or her or similarly significantly affects him or her.

2.   Paragraph 1 shall not apply if the decision:

   a)   is necessary for entering into, or performance of, a contract between the data subject and a data controller;

   b)   is authorised by Union or Member State law to which the controller is subject and which also lays down suitable measures to safeguard the data subject's rights and freedoms and legitimate interests; or

   c)   is based on the data subject's explicit consent.

3.   In the cases referred to in points (a) and (c) of paragraph 2, the data controller shall implement suitable measures to safeguard the data subject's rights and freedoms and legitimate interests, at least the right to obtain human intervention on the part of the controller, to express his or her point of view and to contest the decision.

4. Decisions referred to in paragraph 2 shall not be based on special categories of personal data referred to in Article 9(1), unless point (a) or (g) of Article 9(2) applies and suitable measures to safeguard the data subject's rights and freedoms and legitimate interests are in place.

Relevant Recitals

(71) Profiling
(72) Guidance of the European Data Protection Board regarding profiling
(91) Necessity of a data protection impact assessment

Article 23 Restrictions

1. Union or Member State law to which the data controller or processor is subject may restrict by way of a legislative measure the scope of the obligations and rights provided for in Articles 12 to 22 and Article 34, as well as Article 5 in so far as its provisions correspond to the rights and obligations provided for in Articles 12 to 22, when such a restriction respects the essence of the fundamental rights and freedoms and is a necessary and proportionate measure in a democratic society to safeguard:

   a) national security;
   b) defence;
   c) public security;
   d) the prevention, investigation, detection or prosecution of criminal offences or the execution of criminal penalties, including the safeguarding against and the prevention of threats to public security;
   e) other important objectives of general public interest of the Union or of a Member State, in particular an important economic or financial interest of the Union or of a Member State, including monetary, budgetary and taxation a matters, public health and social security;
   f) the protection of judicial independence and judicial proceedings;
   g) the prevention, investigation, detection and prosecution of breaches of ethics for regulated professions;
   h) a monitoring, inspection or regulatory function connected, even occasionally, to the exercise of official authority in the cases referred to in points (a) to (e) and (g);
   i) the protection of the data subject or the rights and freedoms of others;
   j) the enforcement of civil law claims.

2. In particular, any legislative measure referred to in paragraph 1 shall contain specific provisions at least, where relevant, as to:

   a) the purposes of the processing or categories of processing;
   b) the categories of personal data;

c) the scope of the restrictions introduced;
d) the safeguards to prevent abuse or unlawful access or transfer;
e) the specification of the controller or categories of controllers;
f) the storage periods and the applicable safeguards taking into account the nature, scope and purposes of the processing or categories of processing;
g) the risks to the rights and freedoms of data subjects; and
h) the right of data subjects to be informed about the restriction, unless that may be prejudicial to the purpose of the restriction.

Relevant Recital

(73) Restrictions of rights and principles

CHAPTER IV DATA CONTROLLER AND DATA PROCESSOR

Article 24 Responsibility of the controller

1. Taking into account the nature, scope, context and purposes of processing as well as the risks of varying likelihood and severity for the rights and freedoms of natural persons, the controller shall implement appropriate technical and organisational measures to ensure and to be able to demonstrate that processing is performed in accordance with this Regulation. Those measures shall be reviewed and updated where necessary.
2. Where proportionate in relation to processing activities, the measures referred to in paragraph 1 shall include the implementation of appropriate data protection policies by the controller.
3. Adherence to approved codes of conduct as referred to in Article 40 or approved certification mechanisms as referred to in Article 42 may be used as an element by which to demonstrate compliance with the obligations of the controller.

Relevant Recitals

(74) Responsibility and liability of the controller
(75) Risks to the rights and freedoms of natural persons
(76) Risk assessment
(77) Risk assessment guidelines

Article 25 Data protection by design and by default

1. Taking into account the state of the art, the cost of implementation and the nature, scope, context and purposes of processing as well as the risks of varying

likelihood and severity for rights and freedoms of natural persons posed by the processing, the controller shall, both at the time of the determination of the means for processing and at the time of the processing itself, implement appropriate technical and organisational measures, such as pseudonymisation, which are designed to implement data-protection principles, such as data minimisation, in an effective manner and to integrate the necessary safeguards into the processing in order to meet the requirements of this Regulation and protect the rights of data subjects.

2. The controller shall implement appropriate technical and organisational measures for ensuring that, by default, only personal data which are necessary for each specific purpose of the processing are processed. That obligation applies to the amount of personal data collected, the extent of their processing, the period of their storage and their accessibility. In particular, such measures shall ensure that by default personal data are not made accessible without the individual's intervention to an indefinite number of natural persons.

3. An approved certification mechanism pursuant to Article 42 may be used as an element to demonstrate compliance with the requirements set out in paragraphs 1 and 2 of this Article.

Relevant Recital

(78) Appropriate technical and organisational measures

Article 26 Joint Controllers

1. Where two or more controllers jointly determine the purposes and means of processing, they shall be joint controllers. They shall in a transparent manner determine their respective responsibilities for compliance with the obligations under this Regulation, in particular as regards the exercising of the rights of the data subject and their respective duties to provide the information referred to in Articles 13 and 14, by means of an arrangement between them unless, and in so far as, the respective responsibilities of the controllers are determined by Union or Member State law to which the controllers are subject. The arrangement may designate a contact point for data subjects.

2. The arrangement referred to in paragraph 1 shall duly reflect the respective roles and relationships of the joint controllers vis-à-vis the data subjects. The essence of the arrangement shall be made available to the data subject.

3. Irrespective of the terms of the arrangement referred to in paragraph 1, the data subject may exercise his or her rights under this Regulation in respect of and against each of the controllers.

Relevant Recital

(79) Allocation of the responsibilities

Article 27 Representatives of controllers or processors not established in the Union

1. Where Article 3(2) applies, the controller or the processor shall designate in writing a representative in the Union.
2. The obligation laid down in paragraph 1 of this Article shall not apply to:

   a) processing which is occasional, does not include, on a large scale, processing of special categories of data as referred to in Article 9(1) or processing of personal data relating to criminal convictions and offences referred to in Article 10, and is unlikely to result in a risk to the rights and freedoms of natural persons, taking into account the nature, context, scope and purposes of the processing; or
   b) a public authority or body.

3. The representative shall be established in one of the Member States where the data subjects, whose personal data are processed in relation to the offering of goods or services to them, or whose behaviour is monitored, are.
4. The representative shall be mandated by the controller or processor to be addressed in addition to or instead of the controller or the processor by, in particular, supervisory authorities and data subjects, on all issues related to processing, for the purposes of ensuring compliance with this Regulation.
5. The designation of a representative by the controller or processor shall be without prejudice to legal actions which could be initiated against the controller or the processor themselves.

Relevant Recital

(80) Designation of a representative

Article 28 The Processor

1. Where processing is to be carried out on behalf of a controller, the controller shall use only processors providing sufficient guarantees to implement appropriate technical and organisational measures in such a manner that processing will meet the requirements of this Regulation and ensure the protection of the rights of the data subject.

2. The processor shall not engage another processor without prior specific or general written authorisation of the controller. In the case of general written authorisation, the processor shall inform the controller of any intended changes concerning the addition or replacement of other processors, thereby giving the controller the opportunity to object to such changes.

3. Processing by a processor shall be governed by a contract or other legal act under Union or Member State law, that is binding on the processor with regard to the controller and that sets out the subject-matter and duration of the processing, the nature and purpose of the processing, the type of personal data and categories of data subjects and the obligations and rights of the controller. That contract or other legal act shall stipulate, in particular, that the processor:

   a. processes the personal data only on documented instructions from the controller, including with regard to transfers of personal data to a third country or an international organisation, unless required to do so by Union or Member State law to which the processor is subject; in such a case, the processor shall inform the controller of that legal requirement before processing, unless that law prohibits such information on important grounds of public interest;

   b. ensures that persons authorised to process the personal data have committed themselves to confidentiality or are under an appropriate statutory obligation of confidentiality;

   c. takes all measures required pursuant to Article 32;

   d. respects the conditions referred to in paragraphs 2 and 4 for engaging another processor;

   e. taking into account the nature of the processing, assists the controller by appropriate technical and organisational measures, insofar as this is possible, for the fulfilment of the controller's obligation to respond to requests for exercising the data subject's rights laid down in Chapter III;

   f. assists the controller in ensuring compliance with the obligations pursuant to Articles 32 to 36 taking into account the nature of processing and the information available to the processor;

   g. at the choice of the controller, deletes or returns all the personal data to the controller after the end of the provision of services relating to processing, and deletes existing copies unless Union or Member State law requires storage of the personal data;

   h. makes available to the controller all information necessary to demonstrate compliance with the obligations laid down in this Article and allow for and contribute to audits, including inspections, conducted by the controller or another auditor mandated by the controller.

With regard to point (h) of the first subparagraph, the processor shall immediately inform the controller if, in its opinion, an instruction infringes this Regulation or other Union or Member State data protection provisions.

4. Where a processor engages another processor for carrying out specific processing activities on behalf of the controller, the same data protection obligations as set out in the contract or other legal act between the controller and the processor as referred to in paragraph 3 shall be imposed on that other processor by way of a contract or other legal act under Union or Member State law, in particular providing sufficient guarantees to implement appropriate technical and organisational measures in such a manner that the processing will meet the requirements of this Regulation. Where that other processor fails to fulfil its data protection obligations, the initial processor shall remain fully liable to the controller for the performance of that other processor's obligations.

5. Adherence of a processor to an approved code of conduct as referred to in Article 40 or an approved certification mechanism as referred to in Article 42 may be used as an element by which to demonstrate sufficient guarantees as referred to in paragraphs 1 and 4 of this Article.

6. Without prejudice to an individual contract between the controller and the processor, the contract or the other legal act referred to in paragraphs 3 and 4 of this Article may be based, in whole or in part, on standard contractual clauses referred to in paragraphs 7 and 8 of this Article, including when they are part of a certification granted to the controller or processor pursuant to Articles 42 and 43.

7. The Commission may lay down standard contractual clauses for the matters referred to in paragraph 3 and 4 of this Article and in accordance with the examination procedure referred to in Article 93(2).

8. A supervisory authority may adopt standard contractual clauses for the matters referred to in paragraph 3 and 4 of this Article and in accordance with the consistency mechanism referred to in Article 63.

9. The contract or the other legal act referred to in paragraphs 3 and 4 shall be in writing, including in electronic form.

10. Without prejudice to Articles 82, 83 and 84, if a processor infringes this Regulation by determining the purposes and means of processing, the processor shall be considered to be a controller in respect of that processing.

Relevant Recital

(81) The use of processors

Article 29 Processing under the authority of the controller or processor

The processor and any person acting under the authority of the controller or of the processor, who has access to personal data, shall not process those data except on instructions from the controller, unless required to do so by Union or Member State law.

Article 30 Records of processing Activities

1. Each controller and, where applicable, the controller's representative, shall maintain a record of processing activities under its responsibility. That record shall contain all of the following information:

    a) the name and contact details of the controller and, where applicable, the joint controller, the controller's representative and the data protection officer;
    b) the purposes of the processing;
    c) a description of the categories of data subjects and of the categories of personal data;
    d) the categories of recipients to whom the personal data have been or will be disclosed including recipients in third countries or international organisations;
    e) where applicable, transfers of personal data to a third country or an international organisation, including the identification of that third country or international organisation and, in the case of transfers referred to in the second subparagraph of Article 49(1), the documentation of suitable safeguards;
    f) where possible, the envisaged time limits for erasure of the different categories of data;
    g) where possible, a general description of the technical and organisational security measures referred to in Article 32(1).

2. Each processor and, where applicable, the processor's representative shall maintain a record of all categories of processing activities carried out on behalf of a controller, containing:

    a) the name and contact details of the processor or processors and of each controller on behalf of which the processor is acting, and, where applicable, of the controller's or the processor's representative, and the data protection officer;
    b) the categories of processing carried out on behalf of each controller;
    c) where applicable, transfers of personal data to a third country or an international organisation, including the identification of that third country or international organisation and, in the case of transfers referred to in the second subparagraph of Article 49(1), the documentation of suitable safeguards;
    d) where possible, a general description of the technical and organisational security measures referred to in Article 32(1).

3. The records referred to in paragraphs 1 and 2 shall be in writing, including in electronic form.
4. The controller or the processor and, where applicable, the controller's or the processor's representative, shall make the record available to the supervisory authority on request.

5. The obligations referred to in paragraphs 1 and 2 shall not apply to an enterprise or an organisation employing fewer than 250 persons unless the processing it carries out is likely to result in a risk to the rights and freedoms of data subjects, the processing is not occasional, or the processing includes special categories of data as referred to in Article 9(1) or personal data relating to criminal convictions and offences referred to in Article 10.

Relevant Recitals

(13) Taking account of micro, small and medium-sized enterprises
(82) Record of processing activities

Article 31 Cooperation with the supervisory authority

The controller and the processor and, where applicable, their representatives, shall cooperate, on request, with the supervisory authority in the performance of its tasks.

Relevant Recital

(82) Record of processing activities

Article 32 Security of Processing

1. Taking into account the state of the art, the costs of implementation and the nature, scope, context and purposes of processing as well as the risk of varying likelihood and severity for the rights and freedoms of natural persons, the controller and the processor shall implement appropriate technical and organisational measures to ensure a level of security appropriate to the risk, including inter alia as appropriate:

   a) the pseudonymisation and encryption of personal data;
   b) the ability to ensure the ongoing confidentiality, integrity, availability and resilience of processing systems and services;
   c) the ability to restore the availability and access to personal data in a timely manner in the event of a physical or technical incident;
   d) a process for regularly testing, assessing and evaluating the effectiveness of technical and organisational measures for ensuring the security of the processing.

2. In assessing the appropriate level of security account shall be taken in particular of the risks that are presented by processing, in particular from

accidental or unlawful destruction, loss, alteration, unauthorised disclosure of, or access to personal data transmitted, stored or otherwise processed.

3. Adherence to an approved code of conduct as referred to in Article 40 or an approved certification mechanism as referred to in Article 42 may be used as an element by which to demonstrate compliance with the requirements set out in paragraph 1 of this Article.

4. The controller and processor shall take steps to ensure that any natural person acting under the authority of the controller or the processor who has access to personal data does not process them except on instructions from the controller, unless he or she is required to do so by Union or Member State law.

Relevant Recitals

(75) Risks to the rights and freedoms of natural persons
(76) Risk assessment
(77) Risk assessment guidelines
(78) Appropriate technical and organisational measures
(79) Allocation of the responsibilities
(83) Security of processing

Article 33 Notification of a personal data breach to the supervisory authority

1. In the case of a personal data breach, the controller shall without undue delay and, where feasible, not later than 72 hours after having become aware of it, notify the personal data breach to the supervisory authority competent in accordance with Article 55, unless the personal data breach is unlikely to result in a risk to the rights and freedoms of natural persons. Where the notification to the supervisory authority is not made within 72 hours, it shall be accompanied by reasons for the delay.

2. The processor shall notify the controller without undue delay after becoming aware of a personal data breach.

3. The notification referred to in paragraph 1 shall at least:

    1. describe the nature of the personal data breach including where possible, the categories and approximate number of data subjects concerned and the categories and approximate number of personal data records concerned;

    2. communicate the name and contact details of the data protection officer or other contact point where more information can be obtained;

    3. describe the likely consequences of the personal data breach;

    4. describe the measures taken or proposed to be taken by the controller to address the personal data breach, including, where appropriate, measures to mitigate its possible adverse effects.

4. Where, and in so far as, it is not possible to provide the information at the same time, the information may be provided in phases without undue further delay.
5. The controller shall document any personal data breaches, comprising the facts relating to the personal data breach, its effects and the remedial action taken. That documentation shall enable the supervisory authority to verify compliance with this Article.

Relevant Recitals

(85) Notification obligation of breaches to the supervisory authority
(87) Promptness of reporting/notification
(88) Format and procedures of the notification

Article 34 Communication of a personal data breach to the data subject

1. When the personal data breach is likely to result in a high risk to the rights and freedoms of natural persons, the controller shall communicate the personal data breach to the data subject without undue delay.
2. The communication to the data subject referred to in paragraph 1 of this Article shall describe in clear and plain language the nature of the personal data breach and contain at least the information and measures referred to in points (b), (c) and (d) of Article 33(3).
3. The communication to the data subject referred to in paragraph 1 shall not be required if any of the following conditions are met:

    a) the controller has implemented appropriate technical and organisational protection measures, and those measures were applied to the personal data affected by the personal data breach, in particular those that render the personal data unintelligible to any person who is not authorised to access it, such as encryption;
    b) the controller has taken subsequent measures which ensure that the high risk to the rights and freedoms of data subjects referred to in paragraph 1 is no longer likely to materialise;
    c) it would involve disproportionate effort. In such a case, there shall instead be a public communication or similar measure whereby the data subjects are informed in an equally effective manner.

4. If the controller has not already communicated the personal data breach to the data subject, the supervisory authority, having considered the likelihood of the personal data breach resulting in a high risk, may require it to do so or may decide that any of the conditions referred to in paragraph 3 are met.

Relevant Recitals

(86) Notification of data subjects in case of data breaches
(87) Promptness of reporting/notification
(88) Format and procedures of the notification

Article 35 Data Protection Impact Assessment

1. Where a type of processing in particular using new technologies, and taking into account the nature, scope, context and purposes of the processing, is likely to result in a high risk to the rights and freedoms of natural persons, the controller shall, prior to the processing, carry out an assessment of the impact of the envisaged processing operations on the protection of personal data. A single assessment may address a set of similar processing operations that present similar high risks.

2. The controller shall seek the advice of the data protection officer, where designated, when carrying out a data protection impact assessment.

3. A data protection impact assessment referred to in paragraph 1 shall in particular be required in the case of:

   a) a systematic and extensive evaluation of personal aspects relating to natural persons which is based on automated processing, including profiling, and on which decisions are based that produce legal effects concerning the natural person or similarly significantly affect the natural person;

   b) processing on a large scale of special categories of data referred to in Article 9(1), or of personal data relating to criminal convictions and offences referred to in Article 10; or

   c) a systematic monitoring of a publicly accessible area on a large scale.

4. The supervisory authority shall establish and make public a list of the kind of processing operations which are subject to the requirement for a data protection impact assessment pursuant to paragraph 1. The supervisory authority shall communicate those lists to the Board referred to in Article 68.

5. The supervisory authority may also establish and make public a list of the kind of processing operations for which no data protection impact assessment is required. The supervisory authority shall communicate those lists to the Board.

6. Prior to the adoption of the lists referred to in paragraphs 4 and 5, the competent supervisory authority shall apply the consistency mechanism referred to in Article 63 where such lists involve processing activities which are related to the offering of goods or services to data subjects or to the monitoring of their behaviour in several Member States or may substantially affect the free movement of personal data within the Union.

7. The assessment shall contain at least:

    a) a systematic description of the envisaged processing operations and the purposes of the processing, including, where applicable, the legitimate interest pursued by the controller;

    b) an assessment of the necessity and proportionality of the processing operations in relation to the purposes;

    c) an assessment of the risks to the rights and freedoms of data subjects referred to in paragraph 1; and

    d) the measures envisaged to address the risks, including safeguards, security measures and mechanisms to ensure the protection of personal data and to demonstrate compliance with this Regulation taking into account the rights and legitimate interests of data subjects and other persons concerned.

8. Compliance with approved codes of conduct referred to in Article 40 by the relevant controllers or processors shall be taken into due account in assessing the impact of the processing operations performed by such controllers or processors, in particular for the purposes of a data protection impact assessment.

9. Where appropriate, the controller shall seek the views of data subjects or their representatives on the intended processing, without prejudice to the protection of commercial or public interests or the security of processing operations.

10. Where processing pursuant to point (c) or (e) of Article 6(1) has a legal basis in Union law or in the law of the Member State to which the controller is subject, that law regulates the specific processing operation or set of operations in question, and a data protection impact assessment has already been carried out as part of a general impact assessment in the context of the adoption of that legal basis, paragraphs 1 to 7 shall not apply unless Member States deem it to be necessary to carry out such an assessment prior to processing activities.

11. Where necessary, the controller shall carry out a review to assess if processing is performed in accordance with the data protection impact assessment at least when there is a change of the risk represented by processing operations.

Relevant Recitals

(75) Risks to the rights and freedoms of natural persons
(84) Risk evaluation and impact assessment
(89) Elimination of the general reporting requirement
(90) Data protection impact assessment
(91) Necessity of a data protection impact assessment
(92) Broader data protection impact assessment
(93) Data protection impact assessment at authorities

Article 36 Prior Consultation

1. The controller shall consult the supervisory authority prior to processing where a data protection impact assessment under Article 35 indicates that the processing would result in a high risk in the absence of measures taken by the controller to mitigate the risk.

2. Where the supervisory authority is of the opinion that the intended processing referred to in paragraph 1 would infringe this Regulation, in particular where the controller has insufficiently identified or mitigated the risk, the supervisory authority shall, within period of up to eight weeks of receipt of the request for consultation, provide written advice to the controller and, where applicable to the processor, and may use any of its powers referred to in Article 58. That period may be extended by six weeks, taking into account the complexity of the intended processing. The supervisory authority shall inform the controller and, where applicable, the processor, of any such extension within one month of receipt of the request for consultation together with the reasons for the delay. Those periods may be suspended until the supervisory authority has obtained information it has requested for the purposes of the consultation.

3. When consulting the supervisory authority pursuant to paragraph 1, the controller shall provide the supervisory authority with:

   1. where applicable, the respective responsibilities of the controller, joint controllers and processors involved in the processing, in particular for processing within a group of undertakings;
   2. the purposes and means of the intended processing;
   3. the measures and safeguards provided to protect the rights and freedoms of data subjects pursuant to this Regulation;
   4. where applicable, the contact details of the data protection officer;
   5. the data protection impact assessment provided for in Article 35; and
   6. any other information requested by the supervisory authority.

4. Member States shall consult the supervisory authority during the preparation of a proposal for a legislative measure to be adopted by a national parliament, or of a regulatory measure based on such a legislative measure, which relates to processing.

5. Notwithstanding paragraph 1, Member State law may require controllers to consult with, and obtain prior authorisation from, the supervisory authority in relation to processing by a controller for the performance of a task carried out by the controller in the public interest, including processing in relation to social protection and public health.

Relevant Recitals

(94) Consultation of the supervisory authority
(95) Support by the processor
(96) Consultation of the supervisory authority in the course of a legislative process

Article 37 Designation of the data protection officer

1. The controller and the processor shall designate a data protection officer in any case where:

    a) the processing is carried out by a public authority or body, except for courts acting in their judicial capacity;
    b) the core activities of the controller or the processor consist of processing operations which, by virtue of their nature, their scope and/or their purposes, require regular and systematic monitoring of data subjects on a large scale; or
    c) the core activities of the controller or the processor consist of processing on a large scale of special categories of data pursuant to Article 9 and personal data relating to criminal convictions and offences referred to in Article 10.

2. A group of undertakings may appoint a single data protection officer provided that a data protection officer is easily accessible from each establishment.
3. Where the controller or the processor is a public authority or body, a single data protection officer may be designated for several such authorities or bodies, taking account of their organisational structure and size.
4. In cases other than those referred to in paragraph 1, the controller or processor or associations and other bodies representing categories of controllers or processors may or, where required by Union or Member State law shall, designate a data protection officer. The data protection officer may act for such associations and other bodies representing controllers or processors.
5. The data protection officer shall be designated on the basis of professional qualities and, in particular, expert knowledge of data protection law and practices and the ability to fulfil the tasks referred to in Article 39.
6. The data protection officer may be a staff member of the controller or processor or fulfil the tasks on the basis of a service contract.
7. The controller or the processor shall publish the contact details of the data protection officer and communicate them to the supervisory authority.

Relevant Recital

(97) Data protection officer

Article 38 Position of the data protection officer

1. The controller and the processor shall ensure that the data protection officer is involved, properly and in a timely manner, in all issues which relate to the protection of personal data.
2. The controller and processor shall support the data protection officer in performing the tasks referred to in Article 39 by providing resources necessary

to carry out those tasks and access to personal data and processing operations, and to maintain his or her expert knowledge.

3. The controller and processor shall ensure that the data protection officer does not receive any instructions regarding the exercise of those tasks. He or she shall not be dismissed or penalised by the controller or the processor for performing his tasks. The data protection officer shall directly report to the highest management level of the controller or the processor.

4. Data subjects may contact the data protection officer with regard to all issues related to processing of their personal data and to the exercise of their rights under this Regulation.

5. The data protection officer shall be bound by secrecy or confidentiality concerning the performance of his or her tasks, in accordance with Union or Member State law.

6. The data protection officer may fulfil other tasks and duties. The controller or processor shall ensure that any such tasks and duties do not result in a conflict of interests.

Relevant Recital

(97) Data protection officer

Article 39 Tasks of the data protection officer

1. The data protection officer shall have at least the following tasks:

   a) to inform and advise the controller or the processor and the employees who carry out processing of their obligations pursuant to this Regulation and to other Union or Member State data protection provisions;

   b) to monitor compliance with this Regulation, with other Union or Member State data protection provisions and with the policies of the controller or processor in relation to the protection of personal data, including the assignment of responsibilities, awareness-raising and training of staff involved in processing operations, and the related audits;

   c) to provide advice where requested as regards the data protection impact assessment and monitor its performance pursuant to Article 35;

   d) to cooperate with the supervisory authority;

   e) to act as the contact point for the supervisory authority on issues relating to processing, including the prior consultation referred to in Article 36, and to consult, where appropriate, with regard to any other matter.

2. The data protection officer shall in the performance of his or her tasks have due regard to the risk associated with processing operations, taking into account the nature, scope, context and purposes of processing.

Relevant Recital

(97) Data protection officer

Article 40 Codes of Conduct

1. The Member States, the supervisory authorities, the Board and the Commission shall encourage the drawing up of codes of conduct intended to contribute to the proper application of this Regulation, taking account of the specific features of the various processing sectors and the specific needs of micro, small and medium-sized enterprises.

2. Associations and other bodies representing categories of controllers or processors may prepare codes of conduct, or amend or extend such codes, for the purpose of specifying the application of this Regulation, such as with regard to:

   a) fair and transparent processing;
   b) the legitimate interests pursued by controllers in specific contexts;
   c) the collection of personal data;
   d) the pseudonymisation of personal data;
   e) the information provided to the public and to data subjects;
   f) the exercise of the rights of data subjects;
   g) the information provided to, and the protection of, children, and the manner in which the consent of the holders of parental responsibility over children is to be obtained;
   h) the measures and procedures referred to in Articles 24 and 25 and the measures to ensure security of processing referred to in Article 32;
   i) the notification of personal data breaches to supervisory authorities and the communication of such personal data breaches to data subjects;
   j) the transfer of personal data to third countries or international organisations; or
   k) out-of-court proceedings and other dispute resolution procedures for resolving disputes between controllers and data subjects with regard to processing, without prejudice to the rights of data subjects pursuant to Articles 77 and 79.

3. In addition to adherence by controllers or processors subject to this Regulation, codes of conduct approved pursuant to paragraph 5 of this Article and having general validity pursuant to paragraph 9 of this Article may also be adhered to by controllers or processors that are not subject to this Regulation pursuant to Article 3 in order to provide appropriate safeguards within the framework of personal data transfers to third countries or international organisations under the terms referred to in point (e) of Article 46(2). Such controllers or processors shall make binding and enforceable commitments, via contractual or other legally binding instruments, to apply those appropriate safeguards including with regard to the rights of data subjects.

4. A code of conduct referred to in paragraph 2 of this Article shall contain mechanisms which enable the body referred to in Article 41(1) to carry out the mandatory monitoring of compliance with its provisions by the controllers or processors which undertake to apply it, without prejudice to the tasks and powers of supervisory authorities competent pursuant to Article 55 or 56.

5. Associations and other bodies referred to in paragraph 2 of this Article which intend to prepare a code of conduct or to amend or extend an existing code shall submit the draft code, amendment or extension to the supervisory authority which is competent pursuant to Article 55. The supervisory authority shall provide an opinion on whether the draft code, amendment or extension complies with this Regulation and shall approve that draft code, amendment or extension if it finds that it provides sufficient appropriate safeguards.

6. Where the draft code, or amendment or extension is approved in accordance with paragraph 5, and where the code of conduct concerned does not relate to processing activities in several Member States, the supervisory authority shall register and publish the code.

7. Where a draft code of conduct relates to processing activities in several Member States, the supervisory authority which is competent pursuant to Article 55 shall, before approving the draft code, amendment or extension, submit it in the procedure referred to in Article 63 to the Board which shall provide an opinion on whether the draft code, amendment or extension complies with this Regulation or, in the situation referred to in paragraph 3 of this Article, provides appropriate safeguards.

8. Where the opinion referred to in paragraph 7 confirms that the draft code, amendment or extension complies with this Regulation, or, in the situation referred to in paragraph 3, provides appropriate safeguards, the Board shall submit its opinion to the Commission.

9. The Commission may, by way of implementing acts, decide that the approved code of conduct, amendment or extension submitted to it pursuant to paragraph 8 of this Article have general validity within the Union. Those implementing acts shall be adopted in accordance with the examination procedure set out in Article 93(2).

10. The Commission shall ensure appropriate publicity for the approved codes which have been decided as having general validity in accordance with paragraph 9.

11. The Board shall collate all approved codes of conduct, amendments and extensions in a register and shall make them publicly available by way of appropriate means.

Relevant Recitals

(98) Preparation of codes of conduct by organisations and associations
(99) Consultation of stakeholders and data subjects in the development of codes of conduct

Article 41 Monitoring of approved codes of conduct

1. Without prejudice to the tasks and powers of the competent supervisory authority under Articles 57 and 58, the monitoring of compliance with a code of conduct pursuant to Article 40 may be carried out by a body which has an appropriate level of expertise in relation to the subject-matter of the code and is accredited for that purpose by the competent supervisory authority.

2. A body as referred to in paragraph 1 may be accredited to monitor compliance with a code of conduct where that body has:

   a) demonstrated its independence and expertise in relation to the subject-matter of the code to the satisfaction of the competent supervisory authority;

   b) established procedures which allow it to assess the eligibility of controllers and processors concerned to apply the code, to monitor their compliance with its provisions and to periodically review its operation;

   c) established procedures and structures to handle complaints about infringements of the code or the manner in which the code has been, or is being, implemented by a controller or processor, and to make those procedures and structures transparent to data subjects and the public; and

   d) demonstrated to the satisfaction of the competent supervisory authority that its tasks and duties do not result in a conflict of interests.

3. The competent supervisory authority shall submit the draft criteria for accreditation of a body as referred to in paragraph 1 of this Article to the Board pursuant to the consistency mechanism referred to in Article 63.

4. Without prejudice to the tasks and powers of the competent supervisory authority and the provisions of Chapter VIII, a body as referred to in paragraph 1 of this Article shall, subject to appropriate safeguards, take appropriate action in cases of infringement of the code by a controller or processor, including suspension or exclusion of the controller or processor concerned from the code. It shall inform the competent supervisory authority of such actions and the reasons for taking them.

5. The competent supervisory authority shall revoke the accreditation of a body as referred to in paragraph 1 if the conditions for accreditation are not, or are no longer, met or where actions taken by the body infringe this Regulation.

6. This Article shall not apply to processing carried out by public authorities and bodies.

Article 42 Certification

1. The Member States, the supervisory authorities, the Board and the Commission shall encourage, in particular at Union level, the establishment of data protection certification mechanisms and of data protection seals and marks, for

the purpose of demonstrating compliance with this Regulation of processing operations by controllers and processors. The specific needs of micro, small and medium-sized enterprises shall be taken into account.

2. In addition to adherence by controllers or processors subject to this Regulation, data protection certification mechanisms, seals or marks approved pursuant to paragraph 5 of this Article may be established for the purpose of demonstrating the existence of appropriate safeguards provided by controllers or processors that are not subject to this Regulation pursuant to Article 3 within the framework of personal data transfers to third countries or international organisations under the terms referred to in point (f) of Article 46(2). Such controllers or processors shall make binding and enforceable commitments, via contractual or other legally binding instruments, to apply those appropriate safeguards, including with regard to the rights of data subjects.

3. The certification shall be voluntary and available via a process that is transparent.

4. A certification pursuant to this Article does not reduce the responsibility of the controller or the processor for compliance with this Regulation and is without prejudice to the tasks and powers of the supervisory authorities which are competent pursuant to Article 55 or 56.

5. A certification pursuant to this Article shall be issued by the certification bodies referred to in Article 43 or by the competent supervisory authority, on the basis of criteria approved by that competent supervisory authority pursuant to Article 58(3) or by the Board pursuant to Article 63. Where the criteria are approved by the Board, this may result in a common certification, the European Data Protection Seal.

6. The controller or processor which submits its processing to the certification mechanism shall provide the certification body referred to in Article 43, or where applicable, the competent supervisory authority, with all information and access to its processing activities which are necessary to conduct the certification procedure.

7. Certification shall be issued to a controller or processor for a maximum period of three years and may be renewed, under the same conditions, provided that the relevant requirements continue to be met. Certification shall be withdrawn, as applicable, by the certification bodies referred to in Article 43 or by the competent supervisory authority where the requirements for the certification are not or are no longer met.

8. The Board shall collate all certification mechanisms and data protection seals and marks in a register and shall make them publicly available by any appropriate means.

Relevant Recital

(100) Certification

Article 43 Certification Bodies

1. Without prejudice to the tasks and powers of the competent supervisory authority under Articles 57 and 58, certification bodies which have an appropriate level of expertise in relation to data protection shall, after informing the supervisory authority in order to allow it to exercise its powers pursuant to point (h) of Article 58(2) where necessary, issue and renew certification. Member States shall ensure that those certification bodies are accredited by one or both of the following:

    a) the supervisory authority which is competent pursuant to Article 55 or 56;

    b) the national accreditation body named in accordance with Regulation (EC) No 765/2008 of the European Parliament and of the Council in accordance with EN-ISO/IEC 17065/2012 and with the additional requirements established by the supervisory authority which is competent pursuant to Article 55 or 56.

2. Certification bodies referred to in paragraph 1 shall be accredited in accordance with that paragraph only where they have:

    a) demonstrated their independence and expertise in relation to the subject-matter of the certification to the satisfaction of the competent supervisory authority;

    b) undertaken to respect the criteria referred to in Article 42(5) and approved by the supervisory authority which is competent pursuant to Article 55 or 56 or by the Board pursuant to Article 63;

    c) established procedures for the issuing, periodic review and withdrawal of data protection certification, seals and marks;

    d) established procedures and structures to handle complaints about infringements of the certification or the manner in which the certification has been, or is being, implemented by the controller or processor, and to make those procedures and structures transparent to data subjects and the public; and

    e) demonstrated, to the satisfaction of the competent supervisory authority, that their tasks and duties do not result in a conflict of interests.

3. The accreditation of certification bodies as referred to in paragraphs 1 and 2 of this Article shall take place on the basis of criteria approved by the supervisory authority which is competent pursuant to Article 55 or 56 or by the Board pursuant to Article 63. In the case of accreditation pursuant to point (b) of paragraph 1 of this Article, those requirements shall complement those envisaged in Regulation (EC) No 765/2008 and the technical rules that describe the methods and procedures of the certification bodies.

4. The certification bodies referred to in paragraph 1 shall be responsible for the proper assessment leading to the certification or the withdrawal of such certification without prejudice to the responsibility of the controller or processor for compliance with this Regulation. The accreditation shall be issued for a maximum period of five years and may be renewed on the same conditions provided that the certification body meets the requirements set out in this Article.

5. The certification bodies referred to in paragraph 1 shall provide the competent supervisory authorities with the reasons for granting or withdrawing the requested certification.

6. The requirements referred to in paragraph 3 of this Article and the criteria referred to in Article 42(5) shall be made public by the supervisory authority in an easily accessible form. The supervisory authorities shall also transmit those requirements and criteria to the Board. The Board shall collate all certification mechanisms and data protection seals in a register and shall make them publicly available by any appropriate means.

7. Without prejudice to Chapter VIII, the competent supervisory authority or the national accreditation body shall revoke an accreditation of a certification body pursuant to paragraph 1 of this Article where the conditions for the accreditation are not, or are no longer, met or where actions taken by a certification body infringe this Regulation.

8. The Commission shall be empowered to adopt delegated acts in accordance with Article 92 for the purpose of specifying the requirements to be taken into account for the data protection certification mechanisms referred to in Article 42(1).

9. The Commission may adopt implementing acts laying down technical standards for certification mechanisms and data protection seals and marks, and mechanisms to promote and recognise those certification mechanisms, seals and marks. Those implementing acts shall be adopted in accordance with the examination procedure referred to in Article 93(2).

CHAPTER V TRANSFERS OF PERSONAL DATA TO THIRD COUNTRIES OR INTERNATIONAL ORGANISATIONS

Article 44 General principle for transfers

Any transfer of personal data which are undergoing processing or are intended for processing after transfer to a third country or to an international organisation shall take place only if, subject to the other provisions of this Regulation, the conditions laid down in this Chapter are complied with by the controller and processor, including for onward transfers of personal data from the third country or an international organisation to another third country or to another international organisation. All provisions in this Chapter shall be applied in order to ensure that the level of protection of natural persons guaranteed by this Regulation is not undermined.

Relevant Recitals

(101) General principles for international data transfers
(102) International agreements for an appropriate level of data protection

Article 45 Transfers on the basis of an adequacy decision

1. A transfer of personal data to a third country or an international organisation may take place where the Commission has decided that the third country, a territory or one or more specified sectors within that third country, or the international organisation in question ensures an adequate level of protection. Such a transfer shall not require any specific authorisation.
2. When assessing the adequacy of the level of protection, the Commission shall, in particular, take account of the following elements:

    a) the rule of law, respect for human rights and fundamental freedoms, relevant legislation, both general and sectoral, including concerning public security, defence, national security and criminal law and the access of public authorities to personal data, as well as the implementation of such legislation, data protection rules, professional rules and security measures, including rules for the onward transfer of personal data to another third country or international organisation which are complied with in that country or international organisation, case-law, as well as effective and enforceable data subject rights and effective administrative and judicial redress for the data subjects whose personal data are being transferred;

    b) the existence and effective functioning of one or more independent supervisory authorities in the third country or to which an international organisation is subject, with responsibility for ensuring and enforcing compliance with the data protection rules, including adequate enforcement powers, for assisting and advising the data subjects in exercising their rights and for cooperation with the supervisory authorities of the Member States; and

    c) the international commitments the third country or international organisation concerned has entered into, or other obligations arising from legally binding conventions or instruments as well as from its participation in multilateral or regional systems, in particular in relation to the protection of personal data.

3. The Commission, after assessing the adequacy of the level of protection, may decide, by means of implementing act, that a third country, a territory or one or more specified sectors within a third country, or an international

organisation ensures an adequate level of protection within the meaning of paragraph 2 of this Article. The implementing act shall provide for a mechanism for a periodic review, at least every four years, which shall take into account all relevant developments in the third country or international organisation. The implementing act shall specify its territorial and sectoral application and, where applicable, identify the supervisory authority or authorities referred to in point (b) of paragraph 2 of this Article. The implementing act shall be adopted in accordance with the examination procedure referred to in Article 93(2).

4. The Commission shall, on an ongoing basis, monitor developments in third countries and international organisations that could affect the functioning of decisions adopted pursuant to paragraph 3 of this Article and decisions adopted on the basis of Article 25(6) of Directive 95/46/EC.

5. The Commission shall, where available information reveals, in particular following the review referred to in paragraph 3 of this Article, that a third country, a territory or one or more specified sectors within a third country, or an international organisation no longer ensures an adequate level of protection within the meaning of paragraph 2 of this Article, to the extent necessary, repeal, amend or suspend the decision referred to in paragraph 3 of this Article by means of implementing acts without retro-active effect. Those implementing acts shall be adopted in accordance with the examination procedure referred to in Article 93(2).

    On duly justified imperative grounds of urgency, the Commission shall adopt immediately applicable implementing acts in accordance with the procedure referred to in Article 93(3).

6. The Commission shall enter into consultations with the third country or international organisation with a view to remedying the situation giving rise to the decision made pursuant to paragraph 5.

7. A decision pursuant to paragraph 5 of this Article is without prejudice to transfers of personal data to the third country, a territory or one or more specified sectors within that third country, or the international organisation in question pursuant to Articles 46 to 49.

8. The Commission shall publish in the *Official Journal of the European Union* and on its website a list of the third countries, territories and specified sectors within a third country and international organizations for which it has decided that an adequate level of protection is or is no longer ensured.

9. Decisions adopted by the Commission on the basis of Article 25(6) of Directive 95/46/EC shall remain in force until amended, replaced or repealed by a Commission Decision adopted in accordance with paragraph 3 or 5 of this Article.

Relevant Recitals

(103) Appropriate level of data protection based on an adequacy decision
(104) Criteria for an adequacy decision
(105) Consideration of international agreements for an adequacy decision
(106) Monitoring and periodic review of the level of data protection
(107) Amendment, revocation and suspension of adequacy decisions

Article 46 Transfers subject to appropriate safeguards

1. In the absence of a decision pursuant to Article 45(3), a controller or processor may transfer personal data to a third country or an international organisation only if the controller or processor has provided appropriate safeguards, and on condition that enforceable data subject rights and effective legal remedies for data subjects are available.

2. The appropriate safeguards referred to in paragraph 1 may be provided for, without requiring any specific authorisation from a supervisory authority, by:

    a) a legally binding and enforceable instrument between public authorities or bodies;

    b) binding corporate rules in accordance with Article 47;

    c) standard data protection clauses adopted by the Commission in accordance with the examination procedure referred to in Article 93(2);

    d) standard data protection clauses adopted by a supervisory authority and approved by the Commission pursuant to the examination procedure referred to in Article 93(2);

    e) an approved code of conduct pursuant to Article 40 together with binding and enforceable commitments of the controller or processor in the third country to apply the appropriate safeguards, including as regards data subjects' rights; or

    f) an approved certification mechanism pursuant to Article 42 together with binding and enforceable commitments of the controller or processor in the third country to apply the appropriate safeguards, including as regards data subjects' rights.

3. Subject to the authorisation from the competent supervisory authority, the appropriate safeguards referred to in paragraph 1 may also be provided for, in particular, by:

    a) contractual clauses between the controller or processor and the controller, processor or the recipient of the personal data in the third country or international organisation; or

b)   provisions to be inserted into administrative arrangements between public authorities or bodies which include enforceable and effective data subject rights.

4.   The supervisory authority shall apply the consistency mechanism referred to in Article 63 in the cases referred to in paragraph 3 of this Article.

5.   Authorisations by a Member State or supervisory authority on the basis of Article 26(2) of Directive 95/46/EC shall remain valid until amended, replaced or repealed, if necessary, by that supervisory authority. Decisions adopted by the Commission on the basis of Article 26(4) of Directive 95/46/EC shall remain in force until amended, replaced or repealed, if necessary, by a Commission Decision adopted in accordance with paragraph 2 of this Article.

Relevant Recitals

(108) Appropriate safeguards
(109) Standard data protection clauses

Article 47 Binding corporate rules

1.   The competent supervisory authority shall approve binding corporate rules in accordance with the consistency mechanism set out in Article 63, provided that they:

a.   are legally binding and apply to and are enforced by every member concerned of the group of undertakings, or group of enterprises engaged in a joint economic activity, including their employees;
b.   expressly confer enforceable rights on data subjects with regard to the processing of their personal data; and
c.   fulfil the requirements laid down in paragraph 2.

2.   The binding corporate rules referred to in paragraph 1 shall specify at least:

a.   the structure and contact details of the group of undertakings, or group of enterprises engaged in a joint economic activity and of each of its members;
b.   the data transfers or set of transfers, including the categories of personal data, the type of processing and its purposes, the type of data subjects affected and the identification of the third country or countries in question;
c.   their legally binding nature, both internally and externally;
d.   the application of the general data protection principles, in particular purpose limitation, data minimisation, limited storage periods, data quality, data protection by design and by default, legal basis for processing, processing of special categories of personal data, measures to ensure

data security, and the requirements in respect of onward transfers to bodies not bound by the binding corporate rules;

e. the rights of data subjects in regard to processing and the means to exercise those rights, including the right not to be subject to decisions based solely on automated processing, including profiling in accordance with Article 22, the right to lodge a complaint with the competent supervisory authority and before the competent courts of the Member States in accordance with Article 79, and to obtain redress and, where appropriate, compensation for a breach of the binding corporate rules;

f. the acceptance by the controller or processor established on the territory of a Member State of liability for any breaches of the binding corporate rules by any member concerned not established in the Union; the controller or the processor shall be exempt from that liability, in whole or in part, only if it proves that that member is not responsible for the event giving rise to the damage;

g. how the information on the binding corporate rules, in particular on the provisions referred to in points (d), (e) and (f) of this paragraph is provided to the data subjects in addition to Articles 13 and 14;

h. the tasks of any data protection officer designated in accordance with Article 37 or any other person or entity in charge of the monitoring compliance with the binding corporate rules within the group of undertakings, or group of enterprises engaged in a joint economic activity, as well as monitoring training and complaint-handling;

i. the complaint procedures;

j. the mechanisms within the group of undertakings, or group of enterprises engaged in a joint economic activity for ensuring the verification of compliance with the binding corporate rules. Such mechanisms shall include data protection audits and methods for ensuring corrective actions to protect the rights of the data subject. Results of such verification should be communicated to the person or entity referred to in point (h) and to the board of the controlling undertaking of a group of undertakings, or of the group of enterprises engaged in a joint economic activity, and should be available upon request to the competent supervisory authority;

k. the mechanisms for reporting and recording changes to the rules and reporting those changes to the supervisory authority;

l. the cooperation mechanism with the supervisory authority to ensure compliance by any member of the group of undertakings, or group of enterprises engaged in a joint economic activity, in particular by making available to the supervisory authority the results of verifications of the measures referred to in point (j);

m. the mechanisms for reporting to the competent supervisory authority any legal requirements to which a member of the group of undertakings, or group of enterprises engaged in a joint economic activity is subject in a third country which are likely to have a substantial adverse effect on the guarantees provided by the binding corporate rules; and

n.   the appropriate data protection training to personnel having permanent or regular access to personal data.

3.   The Commission may specify the format and procedures for the exchange of information between controllers, processors and supervisory authorities for binding corporate rules within the meaning of this Article. Those implementing acts shall be adopted in accordance with the examination procedure set out in Article 93(2).

Relevant Recital

(110) Binding corporate rules

Article 48 Transfers or disclosures not authorised by Union law

Any judgment of a court or tribunal and any decision of an administrative authority of a third country requiring a controller or processor to transfer or disclose personal data may only be recognised or enforceable in any manner if based on an international agreement, such as a mutual legal assistance treaty, in force between the requesting third country and the Union or a Member State, without prejudice to other grounds for transfer pursuant to this Chapter.

Relevant Recital

(115) Rules in third countries contrary to the Regulation

Article 49 Derogations for specific situations

1.   In the absence of an adequacy decision pursuant to Article 45(3), or of appropriate safeguards pursuant to Article 46, including binding corporate rules, a transfer or a set of transfers of personal data to a third country or an international organisation shall take place only on one of the following conditions:

1.   the data subject has explicitly consented to the proposed transfer, after having been informed of the possible risks of such transfers for the data subject due to the absence of an adequacy decision and appropriate safeguards;

2. the transfer is necessary for the performance of a contract between the data subject and the controller or the implementation of pre-contractual measures taken at the data subject's request;

3. the transfer is necessary for the conclusion or performance of a contract concluded in the interest of the data subject between the controller and another natural or legal person;

4. the transfer is necessary for important reasons of public interest;

5. the transfer is necessary for the establishment, exercise or defence of legal claims;

6. the transfer is necessary in order to protect the vital interests of the data subject or of other persons, where the data subject is physically or legally incapable of giving consent;

7. the transfer is made from a register which according to Union or Member State law is intended to provide information to the public and which is open to consultation either by the public in general or by any person who can demonstrate a legitimate interest, but only to the extent that the conditions laid down by Union or Member State law for consultation are fulfilled in the particular case.

Where a transfer could not be based on a provision in Article 45 or 46, including the provisions on binding corporate rules, and none of the derogations for a specific situation referred to in the first subparagraph of this paragraph is applicable, a transfer to a third country or an international organisation may take place only if the transfer is not repetitive, concerns only a limited number of data subjects, is necessary for the purposes of compelling legitimate interests pursued by the controller which are not overridden by the interests or rights and freedoms of the data subject, and the controller has assessed all the circumstances surrounding the data transfer and has on the basis of that assessment provided suitable safeguards with regard to the protection of personal data. The controller shall inform the supervisory authority of the transfer. The controller shall, in addition to providing the information referred to in Articles 13 and 14, inform the data subject of the transfer and on the compelling legitimate interests pursued.

2. A transfer pursuant to point (g) of the first subparagraph of paragraph 1 shall not involve the entirety of the personal data or entire categories of the personal data contained in the register. Where the register is intended for consultation by persons having a legitimate interest, the transfer shall be made only at the request of those persons or if they are to be the recipients.

3. Points (a), (b) and (c) of the first subparagraph of paragraph 1 and the second subparagraph thereof shall not apply to activities carried out by public authorities in the exercise of their public powers.

4. The public interest referred to in point (d) of the first subparagraph of paragraph 1 shall be recognised in Union law or in the law of the Member State to which the controller is subject.

5. In the absence of an adequacy decision, Union or Member State law may, for important reasons of public interest, expressly set limits to the transfer of specific categories of personal data to a third country or an international organisation. Member States shall notify such provisions to the Commission.
6. The controller or processor shall document the assessment as well as the suitable safeguards referred to in the second subparagraph of paragraph 1 of this Article in the records referred to in Article 30.

Relevant Recitals

(111) Exceptions for certain cases of international transfers
(112) Data transfers due to important reasons of public interest
(113) Transfers qualified as not repetitive and that only concern a limited number of data subjects
(114) Safeguarding of enforceability of rights and obligations in the absence of an adequacy decision
(115) Rules in third countries contrary to the Regulation

Article 50 International cooperation for the protection of personal data

1. In relation to third countries and international organisations, the Commission and supervisory authorities shall take appropriate steps to:

    a) develop international cooperation mechanisms to facilitate the effective enforcement of legislation for the protection of personal data;
    b) provide international mutual assistance in the enforcement of legislation for the protection of personal data, including through notification, complaint referral, investigative assistance and information exchange, subject to appropriate safeguards for the protection of personal data and other fundamental rights and freedoms;
    c) engage relevant stakeholders in discussion and activities aimed at furthering international cooperation in the enforcement of legislation for the protection of personal data;
    d) promote the exchange and documentation of personal data protection legislation and practice, including on jurisdictional conflicts with third countries.

Relevant Recital

(116) Cooperation among supervisory authorities

CHAPTER VI INDEPENDENT SUPERVISORY AUTHORITIES

Article 51 Supervisory Authority

1. Each Member State shall provide for one or more independent public authorities to be responsible for monitoring the application of this Regulation, in order to protect the fundamental rights and freedoms of natural persons in relation to processing and to facilitate the free flow of personal data within the Union ('supervisory authority').

2. Each supervisory authority shall contribute to the consistent application of this Regulation throughout the Union. For that purpose, the supervisory authorities shall cooperate with each other and the Commission in accordance with Chapter VII.

3. Where more than one supervisory authority is established in a Member State, that Member State shall designate the supervisory authority which is to represent those authorities in the Board and shall set out the mechanism to ensure compliance by the other authorities with the rules relating to the consistency mechanism referred to in Article 63.

4. Each Member State shall notify to the Commission the provisions of its law which it adopts pursuant to this Chapter, by 25 May 2018 and, without delay, any subsequent amendment affecting them.

Relevant Recitals

(117) Establishment of supervisory authorities
(118) Monitoring of the supervisory authorities
(119) Organisation of several supervisory authorities of a Member State
(120) Features of supervisory authorities

Article 52 Independence

1. Each supervisory authority shall act with complete independence in performing its tasks and exercising its powers in accordance with this Regulation.

2. The member or members of each supervisory authority shall, in the performance of their tasks and exercise of their powers in accordance with this Regulation, remain free from external influence, whether direct or indirect, and shall neither seek nor take instructions from anybody.

3. Member or members of each supervisory authority shall refrain from any action incompatible with their duties and shall not, during their term of office, engage in any incompatible occupation, whether gainful or not.

4. Each Member State shall ensure that each supervisory authority is provided with the human, technical and financial resources, premises and infrastructure necessary for the effective performance of its tasks and exercise of its powers, including those to be carried out in the context of mutual assistance, cooperation and participation in the Board.

5. Each Member State shall ensure that each supervisory authority chooses and has its own staff which shall be subject to the exclusive direction of the member or members of the supervisory authority concerned.

6. Each Member State shall ensure that each supervisory authority is subject to financial control which does not affect its independence and that it has separate, public annual budgets, which may be part of the overall state or national budget.

Relevant Recitals

(117) Establishment of supervisory authorities
(118) Monitoring of the supervisory authorities
(120) Features of supervisory authorities
(121) Independence of the supervisory authorities

Article 53 General conditions for the members of the supervisory authority

1. Member States shall provide for each member of their supervisory authorities to be appointed by means of a transparent procedure by:

   – their parliament;
   – their government;
   – their head of State; or
   – an independent body entrusted with the appointment under Member State law.

2. Each member shall have the qualifications, experience and skills, in particular in the area of the protection of personal data, required to perform its duties and exercise its powers.

3. The duties of a member shall end in the event of the expiry of the term of office, resignation or compulsory retirement, in accordance with the law of the Member State concerned.

4. A member shall be dismissed only in cases of serious misconduct or if the member no longer fulfils the conditions required for the performance of the duties.

Relevant Recital

(121) Independence of the supervisory authorities

Article 54 Rules on the establishment of the supervisory authority

1. Each Member State shall provide by law for all of the following:

   a) the establishment of each supervisory authority;

   b) the qualifications and eligibility conditions required to be appointed as member of each supervisory authority;

   c) the rules and procedures for the appointment of the member or members of each supervisory authority;

   d) the duration of the term of the member or members of each supervisory authority of no less than four years, except for the first appointment after 24 May 2016, part of which may take place for a shorter period where that is necessary to protect the independence of the supervisory authority by means of a staggered appointment procedure;

   e) whether and, if so, for how many terms the member or members of each supervisory authority is eligible for reappointment;

   f) the conditions governing the obligations of the member or members and staff of each supervisory authority, prohibitions on actions, occupations and benefits incompatible therewith during and after the term of office and rules governing the cessation of employment.

2. The member or members and the staff of each supervisory authority shall, in accordance with Union or Member State law, be subject to a duty of professional secrecy both during and after their term of office, with regard to any confidential information which has come to their knowledge in the course of the performance of their tasks or exercise of their powers. During their term of office, that duty of professional secrecy shall in particular apply to reporting by natural persons of infringements of this Regulation.

Relevant Recitals

(117) Establishment of supervisory authorities
(121) Independence of the supervisory authorities

Article 55 Competence

1. Each supervisory authority shall be competent for the performance of the tasks assigned to and the exercise of the powers conferred on it in accordance with this Regulation on the territory of its own Member State.

2. Where processing is carried out by public authorities or private bodies acting on the basis of point (c) or (e) of Article 6(1), the supervisory authority of the

Member State concerned shall be competent. In such cases Article 56 does not apply.

3. Supervisory authorities shall not be competent to supervise processing operations of courts acting in their judicial capacity.

Relevant Recital

(122) Responsibility of the supervisory authorities

Article 56 Competence of the lead supervisory authority

1. Without prejudice to Article 55, the supervisory authority of the main establishment or of the single establishment of the controller or processor shall be competent to act as lead supervisory authority for the cross-border processing carried out by that controller or processor in accordance with the procedure provided in Article 60.

2. By derogation from paragraph 1, each supervisory authority shall be competent to handle a complaint lodged with it or a possible infringement of this Regulation, if the subject matter relates only to an establishment in its Member State or substantially affects data subjects only in its Member State.

3. In the cases referred to in paragraph 2 of this Article, the supervisory authority shall inform the lead supervisory authority without delay on that matter. Within a period of three weeks after being informed the lead supervisory authority shall decide whether or not it will handle the case in accordance with the procedure provided in Article 60, taking into account whether or not there is an establishment of the controller or processor in the Member State of which the supervisory authority informed it.

4. Where the lead supervisory authority decides to handle the case, the procedure provided in Article 60 shall apply. The supervisory authority which informed the lead supervisory authority may submit to the lead supervisory authority a draft for a decision. The lead supervisory authority shall take utmost account of that draft when preparing the draft decision referred to in Article 60(3).

5. Where the lead supervisory authority decides not to handle the case, the supervisory authority which informed the lead supervisory authority shall handle it according to Articles 61 and 62.

6. The lead supervisory authority shall be the sole interlocutor of the controller or processor for the cross-border processing carried out by that controller or processor.

Relevant Recitals

(124) Lead authority regarding processing in several Member States
(127) Information of the supervisory authority regarding local processing
(128) Responsibility regarding processing in the public interest

Article 57 Tasks

1. Without prejudice to other tasks set out under this Regulation, each super-
    visory authority shall on its territory:

    a) monitor and enforce the application of this Regulation;
    b) promote public awareness and understanding of the risks, rules, safe-
        guards and rights in relation to processing. Activities addressed specifi-
        cally to children shall receive specific attention;
    c) advise, in accordance with Member State law, the national parliament,
        the government, and other institutions and bodies on legislative and
        administrative measures relating to the protection of natural persons'
        rights and freedoms with regard to processing;
    d) promote the awareness of controllers and processors of their obligations
        under this Regulation;
    e) upon request, provide information to any data subject concerning the
        exercise of their rights under this Regulation and, if appropriate, coop-
        erate with the supervisory authorities in other Member States to that
        end;
    f) handle complaints lodged by a data subject, or by a body, organisation or
        association in accordance with Article 80, and investigate, to the extent
        appropriate, the subject matter of the complaint and inform the com-
        plainant of the progress and the outcome of the investigation within a
        reasonable period, in particular if further investigation or coordination
        with another supervisory authority is necessary;
    g) cooperate with, including sharing information and provide mutual
        assistance to, other supervisory authorities with a view to ensuring the
        consistency of application and enforcement of this Regulation;
    h) conduct investigations on the application of this Regulation, including
        on the basis of information received from another supervisory authority
        or other public authority;
    i) monitor relevant developments, insofar as they have an impact on the
        protection of personal data, in particular the development of information
        and communication technologies and commercial practices;
    j) adopt standard contractual clauses referred to in Article 28(8) and in
        point (d) of Article 46(2);

k) establish and maintain a list in relation to the requirement for data protection impact assessment pursuant to Article 35(4);

l) give advice on the processing operations referred to in Article 36(2);

m) encourage the drawing up of codes of conduct pursuant to Article 40(1) and provide an opinion and approve such codes of conduct which provide sufficient safeguards, pursuant to Article 40(5);

n) encourage the establishment of data protection certification mechanisms and of data protection seals and marks pursuant to Article 42(1), and approve the criteria of certification pursuant to Article 42(5);

o) where applicable, carry out a periodic review of certifications issued in accordance with Article 42(7);

p) draft and publish the criteria for accreditation of a body for monitoring codes of conduct pursuant to Article 41 and of a certification body pursuant to Article 43;

q) conduct the accreditation of a body for monitoring codes of conduct pursuant to Article 41 and of a certification body pursuant to Article 43;

r) authorise contractual clauses and provisions referred to in Article 46(3);

s) approve binding corporate rules pursuant to Article 47;

t) contribute to the activities of the Board;

u) keep internal records of infringements of this Regulation and of measures taken in accordance with Article 58(2); and

v) fulfil any other tasks related to the protection of personal data.

2. Each supervisory authority shall facilitate the submission of complaints referred to in point (f) of paragraph 1 by measures such as a complaint submission form which can also be completed electronically, without excluding other means of communication.

3. The performance of the tasks of each supervisory authority shall be free of charge for the data subject and, where applicable, for the data protection officer.

4. Where requests are manifestly unfounded or excessive, in particular because of their repetitive character, the supervisory authority may charge a reasonable fee based on administrative costs or refuse to act on the request. The supervisory authority shall bear the burden of demonstrating the manifestly unfounded or excessive character of the request.

Relevant Recitals

(122) Responsibility of the supervisory authorities

(123) Cooperation of the supervisory authorities with each other and with the Commission

(132) Awareness-raising activities and specific measures

(133) Mutual assistance and provisional measures

(137) Provisional measures

Article 58 Powers

1. Each supervisory authority shall have all of the following investigative powers:

    a) to order the controller and the processor, and, where applicable, the controller's or the processor's representative to provide any information it requires for the performance of its tasks;

    b) to carry out investigations in the form of data protection audits;

    c) to carry out a review on certifications issued pursuant to Article 42(7);

    d) to notify the controller or the processor of an alleged infringement of this Regulation;

    e) to obtain, from the controller and the processor, access to all personal data and to all information necessary for the performance of its tasks;

    f) to obtain access to any premises of the controller and the processor, including to any data processing equipment and means, in accordance with Union or Member State procedural law.

2. Each supervisory authority shall have all of the following corrective powers:

    a) to issue warnings to a controller or processor that intended processing operations are likely to infringe provisions of this Regulation;

    b) to issue reprimands to a controller or a processor where processing operations have infringed provisions of this Regulation;

    c) to order the controller or the processor to comply with the data subject's requests to exercise his or her rights pursuant to this Regulation;

    d) to order the controller or processor to bring processing operations into compliance with the provisions of this Regulation, where appropriate, in a specified manner and within a specified period;

    e) to order the controller to communicate a personal data breach to the data subject;

    f) to impose a temporary or definitive limitation including a ban on processing;

    g) to order the rectification or erasure of personal data or restriction of processing pursuant to Articles 16, 17 and 18 and the notification of such actions to recipients to whom the personal data have been disclosed pursuant to Article 17(2) and Article 19;

    h) to withdraw a certification or to order the certification body to withdraw a certification issued pursuant to Articles 42 and 43, or to order the certification body not to issue certification if the requirements for the certification are not or are no longer met;

    i) to impose an administrative fine pursuant to Article 83, in addition to, or instead of measures referred to in this paragraph, depending on the circumstances of each individual case;

j) to order the suspension of data flows to a recipient in a third country or to an international organisation.

3. Each supervisory authority shall have all of the following authorisation and advisory powers:

a) to advise the controller in accordance with the prior consultation procedure referred to in Article 36;
b) to issue, on its own initiative or on request, opinions to the national parliament, the Member State government or, in accordance with Member State law, to other institutions and bodies as well as to the public on any issue related to the protection of personal data;
c) to authorise processing referred to in Article 36(5), if the law of the Member State requires such prior authorisation;
d) to issue an opinion and approve draft codes of conduct pursuant to Article 40(5);
e) to accredit certification bodies pursuant to Article 43;
f) to issue certifications and approve criteria of certification in accordance with Article 42(5);
g) to adopt standard data protection clauses referred to in Article 28(8) and in point (d) of Article 46(2);
h) to authorise contractual clauses referred to in point (a) of Article 46(3);
i) to authorise administrative arrangements referred to in point (b) of Article 46(3);
j) to approve binding corporate rules pursuant to Article 47.

4. The exercise of the powers conferred on the supervisory authority pursuant to this Article shall be subject to appropriate safeguards, including effective judicial remedy and due process, set out in Union and Member State law in accordance with the Charter.
5. Each Member State shall provide by law that its supervisory authority shall have the power to bring infringements of this Regulation to the attention of the judicial authorities and where appropriate, to commence or engage otherwise in legal proceedings, in order to enforce the provisions of this Regulation.
6. Each Member State may provide by law that its supervisory authority shall have additional powers to those referred to in paragraphs 1, 2 and 3. The exercise of those powers shall not impair the effective operation of Chapter VII.

Relevant Recitals

(122) Responsibility of the supervisory authorities
(129) Tasks and powers of the supervisory authorities
(131) Attempt of an amicable settlement

Article 59 Activity Reports

Each supervisory authority shall draw up an annual report on its activities, which may include a list of types of infringement notified and types of measures taken in accordance with Article 58(2). Those reports shall be transmitted to the national parliament, the government and other authorities as designated by Member State law. They shall be made available to the public, to the Commission and to the Board.

CHAPTER VII COOPERATION AND CONSISTENCY

Article 60 Cooperation between the lead supervisory authority and the other supervisory authorities concerned

1. The lead supervisory authority shall cooperate with the other supervisory authorities concerned in accordance with this Article in an endeavour to reach consensus. The lead supervisory authority and the supervisory authorities concerned shall exchange all relevant information with each other.
2. The lead supervisory authority may request at any time other supervisory authorities concerned to provide mutual assistance pursuant to Article 61 and may conduct joint operations pursuant to Article 62, in particular for carrying out investigations or for monitoring the implementation of a measure concerning a controller or processor established in another Member State.
3. The lead supervisory authority shall, without delay, communicate the relevant information on the matter to the other supervisory authorities concerned. It shall without delay submit a draft decision to the other supervisory authorities concerned for their opinion and take due account of their views.
4. Where any of the other supervisory authorities concerned within a period of four weeks after having been consulted in accordance with paragraph 3 of this Article, expresses a relevant and reasoned objection to the draft decision, the lead supervisory authority shall, if it does not follow the relevant and reasoned objection or is of the opinion that the objection is not relevant or reasoned, submit the matter to the consistency mechanism referred to in Article 63.
5. Where the lead supervisory authority intends to follow the relevant and reasoned objection made, it shall submit to the other supervisory authorities concerned a revised draft decision for their opinion. That revised draft decision shall be subject to the procedure referred to in paragraph 4 within a period of two weeks.
6. Where none of the other supervisory authorities concerned has objected to the draft decision submitted by the lead supervisory authority within the period referred to in paragraphs 4 and 5, the lead supervisory authority and

the supervisory authorities concerned shall be deemed to be in agreement with that draft decision and shall be bound by it.

7. The lead supervisory authority shall adopt and notify the decision to the main establishment or single establishment of the controller or processor, as the case may be and inform the other supervisory authorities concerned and the Board of the decision in question, including a summary of the relevant facts and grounds. The supervisory authority with which a complaint has been lodged shall inform the complainant on the decision.

8. By derogation from paragraph 7, where a complaint is dismissed or rejected, the supervisory authority with which the complaint was lodged shall adopt the decision and notify it to the complainant and shall inform the controller thereof.

9. Where the lead supervisory authority and the supervisory authorities concerned agree to dismiss or reject parts of a complaint and to act on other parts of that complaint, a separate decision shall be adopted for each of those parts of the matter. The lead supervisory authority shall adopt the decision for the part concerning actions in relation to the controller, shall notify it to the main establishment or single establishment of the controller or processor on the territory of its Member State and shall inform the complainant thereof, while the supervisory authority of the complainant shall adopt the decision for the part concerning dismissal or rejection of that complaint, and shall notify it to that complainant and shall inform the controller or processor thereof.

10. After being notified of the decision of the lead supervisory authority pursuant to paragraphs 7 and 9, the controller or processor shall take the necessary measures to ensure compliance with the decision as regards processing activities in the context of all its establishments in the Union. The controller or processor shall notify the measures taken for complying with the decision to the lead supervisory authority, which shall inform the other supervisory authorities concerned.

11. Where, in exceptional circumstances, a supervisory authority concerned has reasons to consider that there is an urgent need to act in order to protect the interests of data subjects, the urgency procedure referred to in Article 66 shall apply.

12. The lead supervisory authority and the other supervisory authorities concerned shall supply the information required under this Article to each other by electronic means, using a standardised format.

Relevant Recitals

(124) Lead authority regarding processing in several Member States
(125) Competences of the lead authority
(130) Consideration of the authority with which the complaint has been lodged

Article 61 Mutual Assistance

1. Supervisory authorities shall provide each other with relevant information and mutual assistance in order to implement and apply this Regulation in a consistent manner, and shall put in place measures for effective cooperation with one another. Mutual assistance shall cover, in particular, information requests and supervisory measures, such as requests to carry out prior authorisations and consultations, inspections and investigations.

2. Each supervisory authority shall take all appropriate measures required to reply to a request of another supervisory authority without undue delay and no later than one month after receiving the request. Such measures may include, in particular, the transmission of relevant information on the conduct of an investigation.

3. Requests for assistance shall contain all the necessary information, including the purpose of and reasons for the request. Information exchanged shall be used only for the purpose for which it was requested.

4. The requested supervisory authority shall not refuse to comply with the request unless:

    a) it is not competent for the subject-matter of the request or for the measures it is requested to execute; or

    b) compliance with the request would infringe this Regulation or Union or Member State law to which the supervisory authority receiving the request is subject.

5. The requested supervisory authority shall inform the requesting supervisory authority of the results or, as the case may be, of the progress of the measures taken in order to respond to the request. The requested supervisory authority shall provide reasons for any refusal to comply with a request pursuant to paragraph 4.

6. Requested supervisory authorities shall, as a rule, supply the information requested by other supervisory authorities by electronic means, using a standardised format.

7. Requested supervisory authorities shall not charge a fee for any action taken by them pursuant to a request for mutual assistance. Supervisory authorities may agree on rules to indemnify each other for specific expenditure arising from the provision of mutual assistance in exceptional circumstances.

8. Where a supervisory authority does not provide the information referred to in paragraph 5 of this Article within one month of receiving the request of another supervisory authority, the requesting supervisory authority may adopt a provisional measure on the territory of its Member State in accordance with Article 55(1). In that case, the urgent need to act under Article 66(1) shall be presumed to be met and require an urgent binding decision from the Board pursuant to Article 66(2).

9. The Commission may, by means of implementing acts, specify the format and procedures for mutual assistance referred to in this Article and the arrangements for the exchange of information by electronic means between supervisory authorities, and between supervisory authorities and the Board, in particular the standardised format referred to in paragraph 6 of this Article. Those implementing acts shall be adopted in accordance with the examination procedure referred to in Article 93(2).

Relevant Recitals

(123) Cooperation of the supervisory authorities with each other and with the Commission
(132) Awareness-raising activities and specific measures
(133) Mutual assistance and provisional measures

Article 62 Joint operations of supervisory authorities

1. The supervisory authorities shall, where appropriate, conduct joint operations including joint investigations and joint enforcement measures in which members or staff of the supervisory authorities of other Member States are involved.
2. Where the controller or processor has establishments in several Member States or where a significant number of data subjects in more than one Member State are likely to be substantially affected by processing operations, a supervisory authority of each of those Member States shall have the right to participate in joint operations. The supervisory authority which is competent pursuant to Article 56(1) or (4) shall invite the supervisory authority of each of those Member States to take part in the joint operations and shall respond without delay to the request of a supervisory authority to participate.
3. A supervisory authority may, in accordance with Member State law, and with the seconding supervisory authority's authorisation, confer powers, including investigative powers on the seconding supervisory authority's members or staff involved in joint operations or, in so far as the law of the Member State of the host supervisory authority permits, allow the seconding supervisory authority's members or staff to exercise their investigative powers in accordance with the law of the Member State of the seconding supervisory authority. Such investigative powers may be exercised only under the guidance and in the presence of members or staff of the host supervisory authority. The seconding supervisory authority's members or staff shall be subject to the Member State law of the host supervisory authority.
4. Where, in accordance with paragraph 1, staff of a seconding supervisory authority operate in another Member State, the Member State of the host

supervisory authority shall assume responsibility for their actions, including liability, for any damage caused by them during their operations, in accordance with the law of the Member State in whose territory they are operating.

5. The Member State in whose territory the damage was caused shall make good such damage under the conditions applicable to damage caused by its own staff. The Member State of the seconding supervisory authority whose staff has caused damage to any person in the territory of another Member State shall reimburse that other Member State in full any sums it has paid to the persons entitled on their behalf.

6. Without prejudice to the exercise of its rights vis-à-vis third parties and with the exception of paragraph 5, each Member State shall refrain, in the case provided for in paragraph 1, from requesting reimbursement from another Member State in relation to damage referred to in paragraph 4.

7. Where a joint operation is intended and a supervisory authority does not, within one month, comply with the obligation laid down in the second sentence of paragraph 2 of this Article, the other supervisory authorities may adopt a provisional measure on the territory of its Member State in accordance with Article 55. In that case, the urgent need to act under Article 66(1) shall be presumed to be met and require an opinion or an urgent binding decision from the Board pursuant to Article 66(2).

Relevant Recitals

(126) Joint Decisions
(134) Participation in joint operations

Article 63 Consistency Mechanism

In order to contribute to the consistent application of this Regulation throughout the Union, the supervisory authorities shall cooperate with each other and, where relevant, with the Commission, through the consistency mechanism as set out in this Section.

Relevant Recital

(135) Consistency mechanism

Article 64 Opinion of the Board

1. The Board shall issue an opinion where a competent supervisory authority intends to adopt any of the measures below. To that end, the competent supervisory authority shall communicate the draft decision to the Board, when it:

a) aims to adopt a list of the processing operations subject to the requirement for a data protection impact assessment pursuant to Article 35(4);

b) concerns a matter pursuant to Article 40(7) whether a draft code of conduct or an amendment or extension to a code of conduct complies with this Regulation;

c) aims to approve the criteria for accreditation of a body pursuant to Article 41(3) or a certification body pursuant to Article 43(3);

d) aims to determine standard data protection clauses referred to in point (d) of Article 46(2) and in Article 28(8);

e) aims to authorise contractual clauses referred to in point (a) of Article 46(3); or

f) aims to approve binding corporate rules within the meaning of Article 47.

2. Any supervisory authority, the Chair of the Board or the Commission may request that any matter of general application or producing effects in more than one Member State be examined by the Board with a view to obtaining an opinion, in particular where a competent supervisory authority does not comply with the obligations for mutual assistance in accordance with Article 61 or for joint operations in accordance with Article 62.

3. In the cases referred to in paragraphs 1 and 2, the Board shall issue an opinion on the matter submitted to it provided that it has not already issued an opinion on the same matter. That opinion shall be adopted within eight weeks by simple majority of the members of the Board. That period may be extended by a further six weeks, taking into account the complexity of the subject matter. Regarding the draft decision referred to in paragraph 1 circulated to the members of the Board in accordance with paragraph 5, a member which has not objected within a reasonable period indicated by the Chair, shall be deemed to be in agreement with the draft decision.

4. Supervisory authorities and the Commission shall, without undue delay, communicate by electronic means to the Board, using a standardised format any relevant information, including as the case may be a summary of the facts, the draft decision, the grounds which make the enactment of such measure necessary, and the views of other supervisory authorities concerned.

5. The Chair of the Board shall, without undue, delay inform by electronic means:

a) the members of the Board and the Commission of any relevant information which has been communicated to it using a standardised format. The secretariat of the Board shall, where necessary, provide translations of relevant information; and

b) the supervisory authority referred to, as the case may be, in paragraphs 1 and 2, and the Commission of the opinion and make it public.

6. The competent supervisory authority shall not adopt its draft decision referred to in paragraph 1 within the period referred to in paragraph 3.

7. The supervisory authority referred to in paragraph 1 shall take utmost account of the opinion of the Board and shall, within two weeks after receiving the opinion, communicate to the Chair of the Board by electronic means whether it will maintain or amend its draft decision and, if any, the amended draft decision, using a standardised format.

8. Where the supervisory authority concerned informs the Chair of the Board within the period referred to in paragraph 7 of this Article that it does not intend to follow the opinion of the Board, in whole or in part, providing the relevant grounds, Article 65(1) shall apply.

Relevant Recital

(136) Binding decisions and opinions of the Board

Article 65 Dispute resolution by the Board

1. In order to ensure the correct and consistent application of this Regulation in individual cases, the Board shall adopt a binding decision in the following cases:

   a) where, in a case referred to in Article 60(4), a supervisory authority concerned has raised a relevant and reasoned objection to a draft decision of the lead authority or the lead authority has rejected such an objection as being not relevant or reasoned. The binding decision shall concern all the matters which are the subject of the relevant and reasoned objection, in particular whether there is an infringement of this Regulation;

   b) where there are conflicting views on which of the supervisory authorities concerned is competent for the main establishment;

   c) where a competent supervisory authority does not request the opinion of the Board in the cases referred to in Article 64(1), or does not follow the opinion of the Board issued under Article 64. In that case, any supervisory authority concerned or the Commission may communicate the matter to the Board.

2. The decision referred to in paragraph 1 shall be adopted within one month from the referral of the subject-matter by a two-thirds majority of the members of the Board. That period may be extended by a further month on account of the complexity of the subject-matter. The decision referred to in paragraph 1 shall be reasoned and addressed to the lead supervisory authority and all the supervisory authorities concerned and binding on them.

3. Where the Board has been unable to adopt a decision within the periods referred to in paragraph 2, it shall adopt its decision within two weeks following the expiration of the second month referred to in paragraph 2 by a

simple majority of the members of the Board. Where the members of the Board are split, the decision shall by adopted by the vote of its Chair.

4. The supervisory authorities concerned shall not adopt a decision on the subject-matter submitted to the Board under paragraph 1 during the periods referred to in paragraphs 2 and 3.

5. The Chair of the Board shall notify, without undue delay, the decision referred to in paragraph 1 to the supervisory authorities concerned. It shall inform the Commission thereof. The decision shall be published on the website of the Board without delay after the supervisory authority has notified the final decision referred to in paragraph 6.

6. The lead supervisory authority or, as the case may be, the supervisory authority with which the complaint has been lodged shall adopt its final decision on the basis of the decision referred to in paragraph 1 of this Article, without undue delay and at the latest by one month after the Board has notified its decision. The lead supervisory authority or, as the case may be, the supervisory authority with which the complaint has been lodged, shall inform the Board of the date when its final decision is notified respectively to the controller or the processor and to the data subject. The final decision of the supervisory authorities concerned shall be adopted under the terms of Article 60(7), (8) and (9). The final decision shall refer to the decision referred to in paragraph 1 of this Article and shall specify that the decision referred to in that paragraph will be published on the website of the Board in accordance with paragraph 5 of this Article. The final decision shall attach the decision referred to in paragraph 1 of this Article.

Relevant Recital

(136) Binding decisions and opinions of the Board

Article 66 Urgency Procedure

1. In exceptional circumstances, where a supervisory authority concerned considers that there is an urgent need to act in order to protect the rights and freedoms of data subjects, it may, by way of derogation from the consistency mechanism referred to in Articles 63, 64 and 65 or the procedure referred to in Article 60, immediately adopt provisional measures intended to produce legal effects on its own territory with a specified period of validity which shall not exceed three months. The supervisory authority shall, without delay, communicate those measures and the reasons for adopting them to the other supervisory authorities concerned, to the Board and to the Commission.

2. Where a supervisory authority has taken a measure pursuant to paragraph 1 and considers that final measures need urgently be adopted, it may request an

urgent opinion or an urgent binding decision from the Board, giving reasons for requesting such opinion or decision.

3. Any supervisory authority may request an urgent opinion or an urgent binding decision, as the case may be, from the Board where a competent supervisory authority has not taken an appropriate measure in a situation where there is an urgent need to act, in order to protect the rights and freedoms of data subjects, giving reasons for requesting such opinion or decision, including for the urgent need to act.

4. By derogation from Article 64(3) and Article 65(2), an urgent opinion or an urgent binding decision referred to in paragraphs 2 and 3 of this Article shall be adopted within two weeks by simple majority of the members of the Board.

Relevant Recitals

(137) Provisional measures
(138) Urgency procedure

Article 67 Exchange of Information

The Commission may adopt implementing acts of general scope in order to specify the arrangements for the exchange of information by electronic means between supervisory authorities, and between supervisory authorities and the Board, in particular the standardised format referred to in Article 64.

Those implementing acts shall be adopted in accordance with the examination procedure referred to in Article 93(2).

Article 68 European Data Protection Board

1. The European Data Protection Board (the 'Board') is hereby established as a body of the Union and shall have legal personality.

2. The Board shall be represented by its Chair.

3. The Board shall be composed of the head of one supervisory authority of each Member State and of the European Data Protection Supervisor, or their respective representatives.

4. Where in a Member State more than one supervisory authority is responsible for monitoring the application of the provisions pursuant to this Regulation, a joint representative shall be appointed in accordance with that Member State's law.

5. The Commission shall have the right to participate in the activities and meetings of the Board without voting right. The Commission shall designate a representative. The Chair of the Board shall communicate to the Commission the activities of the Board.

6. In the cases referred to in Article 65, the European Data Protection Supervisor shall have voting rights only on decisions which concern principles and rules applicable to the Union institutions, bodies, offices and agencies which correspond in substance to those of this Regulation.

Relevant Recital

(139) European Data Protection Board

Article 69 Independence

1. The Board shall act independently when performing its tasks or exercising its powers pursuant to Articles 70 and 71.
2. Without prejudice to requests by the Commission referred to in point (b) of Article 70(1) and in Article 70(2), the Board shall, in the performance of its tasks or the exercise of its powers, neither seek nor take instructions from anybody.

Relevant Recital

(139) European Data Protection Board

Article 70 Tasks of the Board

1. The Board shall ensure the consistent application of this Regulation. To that end, the Board shall, on its own initiative or, where relevant, at the request of the Commission, in particular:

   a) monitor and ensure the correct application of this Regulation in the cases provided for in Articles 64 and 65 without prejudice to the tasks of national supervisory authorities;

   b) advise the Commission on any issue related to the protection of personal data in the Union, including on any proposed amendment of this Regulation;

   c) advise the Commission on the format and procedures for the exchange of information between controllers, processors and supervisory authorities for binding corporate rules;

   d) issue guidelines, recommendations, and best practices on procedures for erasing links, copies or replications of personal data from publicly available communication services as referred to in Article 17(2);

   e) examine, on its own initiative, on request of one of its members or on request of the Commission, any question covering the application of this Regulation and issue guidelines, recommendations and best practices in order to encourage consistent application of this Regulation;

f)   issue guidelines, recommendations and best practices in accordance with point (e) of this paragraph for further specifying the criteria and conditions for decisions based on profiling pursuant to Article 22(1);

g)   issue guidelines, recommendations and best practices in accordance with point (e) of this paragraph for establishing the personal data breaches and determining the undue delay referred to in Article 33(1) and (2) and for the particular circumstances in which a controller or a processor is required to notify the personal data breach;

h)   issue guidelines, recommendations and best practices in accordance with point (e) of this paragraph as to the circumstances in which a personal data breach is likely to result in a high risk to the rights and freedoms of the natural persons referred to in Article 34(1);

i)   issue guidelines, recommendations and best practices in accordance with point (e) of this paragraph for the purpose of further specifying the criteria and requirements for personal data transfers based on binding corporate rules adhered to by controllers and binding corporate rules adhered to by processors and on further necessary requirements to ensure the protection of personal data of the data subjects concerned referred to in Article 47;

j)   issue guidelines, recommendations and best practices in accordance with point (e) of this paragraph for the purpose of further specifying the criteria and requirements for the personal data transfers on the basis of Article 49(1);

k)   draw up guidelines for supervisory authorities concerning the application of measures referred to in Article 58(1), (2) and (3) and the setting of administrative fines pursuant to Article 83;

l)   review the practical application of the guidelines, recommendations and best practices referred to in points (e) and (f);

m)   issue guidelines, recommendations and best practices in accordance with point (e) of this paragraph for establishing common procedures for reporting by natural persons of infringements of this Regulation pursuant to Article 54(2);

n)   encourage the drawing-up of codes of conduct and the establishment of data protection certification mechanisms and data protection seals and marks pursuant to Articles 40 and 42;

o)   carry out the accreditation of certification bodies and its periodic review pursuant to Article 43 and maintain a public register of accredited bodies pursuant to Article 43(6) and of the accredited controllers or processors established in third countries pursuant to Article 42(7);

p)   specify the requirements referred to in Article 43(3) with a view to the accreditation of certification bodies under Article 42;

q)   provide the Commission with an opinion on the certification requirements referred to in Article 43(8);

r) provide the Commission with an opinion on the icons referred to in Article 12(7);

s) provide the Commission with an opinion for the assessment of the adequacy of the level of protection in a third country or international organisation, including for the assessment whether a third country, a territory or one or more specified sectors within that third country, or an international organisation no longer ensures an adequate level of protection. To that end, the Commission shall provide the Board with all necessary documentation, including correspondence with the government of the third country, with regard to that third country, territory or specified sector, or with the international organisation;

t) issue opinions on draft decisions of supervisory authorities pursuant to the consistency mechanism referred to in Article 64(1), on matters submitted pursuant to Article 64(2) and to issue binding decisions pursuant to Article 65, including in cases referred to in Article 66;

u) promote the cooperation and the effective bilateral and multilateral exchange of information and best practices between the supervisory authorities;

v) promote common training programmes and facilitate personnel exchanges between the supervisory authorities and, where appropriate, with the supervisory authorities of third countries or with international organisations;

w) promote the exchange of knowledge and documentation on data protection legislation and practice with data protection supervisory authorities worldwide;

x) issue opinions on codes of conduct drawn up at Union level pursuant to Article 40(9); and

y) maintain a publicly accessible electronic register of decisions taken by supervisory authorities and courts on issues handled in the consistency mechanism.

2. Where the Commission requests advice from the Board, it may indicate a time limit, taking into account the urgency of the matter.

3. The Board shall forward its opinions, guidelines, recommendations, and best practices to the Commission and to the committee referred to in Article 93 and make them public.

4. The Board shall, where appropriate, consult interested parties and give them the opportunity to comment within a reasonable period. The Board shall, without prejudice to Article 76, make the results of the consultation procedure publicly available.

Relevant Recitals

(136) Binding decisions and opinions of the Board
(139) European Data Protection Board

Article 71 Reports

1. The Board shall draw up an annual report regarding the protection of natural persons with regard to processing in the Union and, where relevant, in third countries and international organisations. The report shall be made public and be transmitted to the European Parliament, to the Council and to the Commission.
2. The annual report shall include a review of the practical application of the guidelines, recommendations and best practices referred to in point (l) of Article 70(1) as well as of the binding decisions referred to in Article 65.

Article 72 Procedure

1. The Board shall take decisions by a simple majority of its members, unless otherwise provided for in this Regulation.
2. The Board shall adopt its own rules of procedure by a two-thirds majority of its members and organise its own operational arrangements.

Article 73 Chair

1. The Board shall elect a chair and two deputy chairs from amongst its members by simple majority.
2. The term of office of the Chair and of the deputy chairs shall be five years and be renewable once.

Article 74 Tasks of the Chair

1. The Chair shall have the following tasks:

    a) to convene the meetings of the Board and prepare its agenda;
    b) to notify decisions adopted by the Board pursuant to Article 65 to the lead supervisory authority and the supervisory authorities concerned;
    c) to ensure the timely performance of the tasks of the Board, in particular in relation to the consistency mechanism referred to in Article 63.

2. The Board shall lay down the allocation of tasks between the Chair and the deputy chairs in its rules of procedure.

Article 75 Secretariat

1. The Board shall have a secretariat, which shall be provided by the European Data Protection Supervisor.
2. The secretariat shall perform its tasks exclusively under the instructions of the Chair of the Board.
3. The staff of the European Data Protection Supervisor involved in carrying out the tasks conferred on the Board by this Regulation shall be subject to separate reporting lines from the staff involved in carrying out tasks conferred on the European Data Protection Supervisor.
4. Where appropriate, the Board and the European Data Protection Supervisor shall establish and publish a Memorandum of Understanding implementing this Article, determining the terms of their cooperation, and applicable to the staff of the European Data Protection Supervisor involved in carrying out the tasks conferred on the Board by this Regulation.
5. The secretariat shall provide analytical, administrative and logistical support to the Board.
6. The secretariat shall be responsible in particular for:

   a) the day-to-day business of the Board;
   b) communication between the members of the Board, its Chair and the Commission;
   c) communication with other institutions and the public;
   d) the use of electronic means for the internal and external communication;
   e) the translation of relevant information;
   f) the preparation and follow-up of the meetings of the Board;
   g) the preparation, drafting and publication of opinions, decisions on the settlement of disputes between supervisory authorities and other texts adopted by the Board.

Relevant Recital

(140) Secretariat and staff of the Board

Article 76 Confidentiality

1. The discussions of the Board shall be confidential where the Board deems it necessary, as provided for in its rules of procedure.

2. Access to documents submitted to members of the Board, experts and representatives of third parties shall be governed by Regulation (EC) No 1049/2001 of the European Parliament and of the Council.

CHAPTER VIII REMEDIES, LIABILITY AND PENALTIES

Article 77 Right to lodge a complaint with a supervisory authority

1. Without prejudice to any other administrative or judicial remedy, every data subject shall have the right to lodge a complaint with a supervisory authority, in particular in the Member State of his or her habitual residence, place of work or place of the alleged infringement if the data subject considers that the processing of personal data relating to him or her infringes this Regulation.
2. The supervisory authority with which the complaint has been lodged shall inform the complainant on the progress and the outcome of the complaint including the possibility of a judicial remedy pursuant to Article 78.

Relevant Recital

(141) Right of Appeal

Article 78 Right to an effective judicial remedy against a supervisory authority

1. Without prejudice to any other administrative or non-judicial remedy, each natural or legal person shall have the right to an effective judicial remedy against a legally binding decision of a supervisory authority concerning them.
2. Without prejudice to any other administrative or non-judicial remedy, each data subject shall have the right to a an effective judicial remedy where the supervisory authority which is competent pursuant to Articles 55 and 56 does not handle a complaint or does not inform the data subject within three months on the progress or outcome of the complaint lodged pursuant to Article 77.
3. Proceedings against a supervisory authority shall be brought before the courts of the Member State where the supervisory authority is established.
4. Where proceedings are brought against a decision of a supervisory authority which was preceded by an opinion or a decision of the Board in the consistency mechanism, the supervisory authority shall forward that opinion or decision to the court.

Relevant Recitals

(141) Right of Appeal
(143) Judicial remedies

Article 79 Right to an effective judicial remedy against a controller or processor

1.   Without prejudice to any available administrative or non-judicial remedy, including the right to lodge a complaint with a supervisory authority pursuant to Article 77, each data subject shall have the right to an effective judicial remedy where he or she considers that his or her rights under this Regulation have been infringed as a result of the processing of his or her personal data in non-compliance with this Regulation.
2.   Proceedings against a controller or a processor shall be brought before the courts of the Member State where the controller or processor has an establishment. Alternatively, such proceedings may be brought before the courts of the Member State where the data subject has his or her habitual residence, unless the controller or processor is a public authority of a Member State acting in the exercise of its public powers.

Relevant Recitals

(141) Right of Appeal
(145) Choice of venue

Article 80 Representation of data subjects

1.   The data subject shall have the right to mandate a not-for-profit body, organisation or association which has been properly constituted in accordance with the law of a Member State, has statutory objectives which are in the public interest, and is active in the field of the protection of data subjects' rights and freedoms with regard to the protection of their personal data to lodge the complaint on his or her behalf, to exercise the rights referred to in Articles 77, 78 and 79 on his or her behalf, and to exercise the right to receive compensation referred to in Article 82 on his or her behalf where provided for by Member State law.
2.   Member States may provide that any body, organisation or association referred to in paragraph 1 of this Article, independently of a data subject's mandate, has the right to lodge, in that Member State, a complaint with the supervisory authority which is competent pursuant to Article 77 and to exercise the rights

referred to in Articles 78 and 79 if it considers that the rights of a data subject under this Regulation have been infringed as a result of the processing.

Relevant Recital

(142) The right of data subjects to mandate a not-for-profit body, organisation or association.

Article 81 Suspension of Proceedings

1. Where a competent court of a Member State has information on proceedings, concerning the same subject matter as regards processing by the same controller or processor, that are pending in a court in another Member State, it shall contact that court in the other Member State to confirm the existence of such proceedings.
2. Where proceedings concerning the same subject matter as regards processing of the same controller or processor are pending in a court in another Member State, any competent court other than the court first seized may suspend its proceedings.
3. Where those proceedings are pending at first instance, any court other than the court first seized may also, on the application of one of the parties, decline jurisdiction if the court first seized has jurisdiction over the actions in question and its law permits the consolidation thereof.

Relevant Recital

(144) Related proceedings

Article 82 Right to compensation and liability

1. Any person who has suffered material or non-material damage as a result of an infringement of this Regulation shall have the right to receive compensation from the controller or processor for the damage suffered.
2. Any controller involved in processing shall be liable for the damage caused by processing which infringes this Regulation. A processor shall be liable for the damage caused by processing only where it has not complied with obligations of this Regulation specifically directed to processors or where it has acted outside or contrary to lawful instructions of the controller.
3. A controller or processor shall be exempt from liability under paragraph 2 if it proves that it is not in any way responsible for the event giving rise to the damage.
4. Where more than one controller or processor, or both a controller and a processor, are involved in the same processing and where they are, under

    paragraphs 2 and 3, responsible for any damage caused by processing, each controller or processor shall be held liable for the entire damage in order to ensure effective compensation of the data subject.

5. Where a controller or processor has, in accordance with paragraph 4, paid full compensation for the damage suffered, that controller or processor shall be entitled to claim back from the other controllers or processors involved in the same processing that part of the compensation corresponding to their part of responsibility for the damage, in accordance with the conditions set out in paragraph 2.

6. Court proceedings for exercising the right to receive compensation shall be brought before the courts competent under the law of the Member State referred to in Article 79(2).

Relevant Recitals

(146) Indemnity
(147) Jurisdiction

Article 83 General conditions for imposing administrative fines

1. Each supervisory authority shall ensure that the imposition of administrative fines pursuant to this Article in respect of infringements of this Regulation referred to in paragraphs 4, 5 and 6 shall in each individual case be effective, proportionate and dissuasive.

2. Administrative fines shall, depending on the circumstances of each individual case, be imposed in addition to, or instead of, measures referred to in points (a) to (h) and (j) of Article 58(2). When deciding whether to impose an administrative fine and deciding on the amount of the administrative fine in each individual case due regard shall be given to the following:

    a)   the nature, gravity and duration of the infringement taking into account the nature, scope or purpose of the processing concerned as well as the number of data subjects affected and the level of damage suffered by them;

    b)   the intentional or negligent character of the infringement;

    c)   any action taken by the controller or processor to mitigate the damage suffered by data subjects;

    d)   the degree of responsibility of the controller or processor taking into account technical and organisational measures implemented by them pursuant to Articles 25 and 32;

    e)   any relevant previous infringements by the controller or processor;

    f)   the degree of cooperation with the supervisory authority, in order to remedy the infringement and mitigate the possible adverse effects of the infringement;

    g)   the categories of personal data affected by the infringement;

h) the manner in which the infringement became known to the supervisory authority, in particular whether, and if so to what extent, the controller or processor notified the infringement;

i) where measures referred to in Article 58(2) have previously been ordered against the controller or processor concerned with regard to the same subject-matter, compliance with those measures;

j) adherence to approved codes of conduct pursuant to Article 40 or approved certification mechanisms pursuant to Article 42; and

k) any other aggravating or mitigating factor applicable to the circumstances of the case, such as financial benefits gained, or losses avoided, directly or indirectly, from the infringement.

3. If a controller or processor intentionally or negligently, for the same or linked processing operations, infringes several provisions of this Regulation, the total amount of the administrative fine shall not exceed the amount specified for the gravest infringement.

4. Infringements of the following provisions shall, in accordance with paragraph 2, be subject to administrative fines up to 10 000 000 EUR, or in the case of an undertaking, up to 2 % of the total worldwide annual turnover of the preceding financial year, whichever is higher:

a) the obligations of the controller and the processor pursuant to Articles 8, 11, 25 to 39 and 42 and 43;

b) the obligations of the certification body pursuant to Articles 42 and 43;

c) the obligations of the monitoring body pursuant to Article 41(4).

5. Infringements of the following provisions shall, in accordance with paragraph 2, be subject to administrative fines up to 20 000 000 EUR, or in the case of an undertaking, up to 4 % of the total worldwide annual turnover of the preceding financial year, whichever is higher:

a) the basic principles for processing, including conditions for consent, pursuant to Articles 5, 6, 7 and 9;

b) the data subjects' rights pursuant to Articles 12 to 22;

c) the transfers of personal data to a recipient in a third country or an international organisation pursuant to Articles 44 to 49;

d) any obligations pursuant to Member State law adopted under Chapter IX;

e) non-compliance with an order or a temporary or definitive limitation on processing or the suspension of data flows by the supervisory authority pursuant to Article 58(2) or failure to provide access in violation of Article 58(1).

6. Non-compliance with an order by the supervisory authority as referred to in Article 58(2) shall, in accordance with paragraph 2 of this Article, be subject

to administrative fines up to 20 000 000 EUR, or in the case of an undertaking, up to 4 % of the total worldwide annual turnover of the preceding financial year, whichever is higher.

7. Without prejudice to the corrective powers of supervisory authorities pursuant to Article 58(2), each Member State may lay down the rules on whether and to what extent administrative fines may be imposed on public authorities and bodies established in that Member State.

8. The exercise by the supervisory authority of its powers under this Article shall be subject to appropriate procedural safeguards in accordance with Union and Member State law, including effective judicial remedy and due process.

9. Where the legal system of the Member State does not provide for administrative fines, this Article may be applied in such a manner that the fine is initiated by the competent supervisory authority and imposed by competent national courts, while ensuring that those legal remedies are effective and have an equivalent effect to the administrative fines imposed by supervisory authorities. In any event, the fines imposed shall be effective, proportionate and dissuasive. Those Member States shall notify to the Commission the provisions of their laws which they adopt pursuant to this paragraph by 25 May 2018 and, without delay, any subsequent amendment law or amendment affecting them.

Relevant Recitals

(148) Penalties
(149) Penalties for infringements of national rules
(150) Administrative fines
(151) Administrative fines in Denmark and Estonia
(152) Power of sanction of the Member States

Article 84 Penalties

1. Member States shall lay down the rules on other penalties applicable to infringements of this Regulation in particular for infringements which are not subject to administrative fines pursuant to Article 83, and shall take all measures necessary to ensure that they are implemented. Such penalties shall be effective, proportionate and dissuasive.

2. Each Member State shall notify to the Commission the provisions of its law which it adopts pursuant to paragraph 1, by ... [*two years from the date of entry into force of this Regulation*] and, without delay, any subsequent amendment affecting them.

CHAPTER IX PROVISIONS RELATING TO SPECIFIC PROCESSING SITUATIONS

Article 85 Processing and freedom of expression and information

1. Member States shall by law reconcile the right to the protection of personal data pursuant to this Regulation with the right to freedom of expression and information, including processing for journalistic purposes and the purposes of academic, artistic or literary expression.
2. For processing carried out for journalistic purposes or the purpose of academic artistic or literary expression, Member States shall provide for exemptions or derogations from Chapter II (principles), Chapter III (rights of the data subject), Chapter IV (controller and processor), Chapter V (transfer of personal data to third countries or international organisations), Chapter VI (independent supervisory authorities), Chapter VII (cooperation and consistency) and Chapter IX (specific data processing situations) if they are necessary to reconcile the right to the protection of personal data with the freedom of expression and information.
3. Each Member State shall notify to the Commission the provisions of its law which it has adopted pursuant to paragraph 2 and, without delay, any subsequent amendment law or amendment affecting them.

Relevant Recital

(153) Processing of personal data solely for journalistic purposes or for the purposes of academic, artistic or literary expression

Article 86 Processing and public access to official documents

Personal data in official documents held by a public authority or a public body or a private body for the performance of a task carried out in the public interest may be disclosed by the authority or body in accordance with Union or Member State law to which the public authority or body is subject in order to reconcile public access to official documents with the right to the protection of personal data pursuant to this Regulation.

Relevant Recital

(154) Principle of public access to official documents

Article 87 Processing of the national identification number

Member States may further determine the specific conditions for the processing of a national identification number or any other identifier of general application. In that case the national identification number or any other identifier of general application shall be used only under appropriate safeguards for the rights and freedoms of the data subject pursuant to this Regulation.

Article 88 Processing in the context of employment

1. Member States may, by law or by collective agreements, provide for more specific rules to ensure the protection of the rights and freedoms in respect of the processing of employees' personal data in the employment context, in particular for the purposes of the recruitment, the performance of the contract of employment, including discharge of obligations laid down by law or by collective agreements, management, planning and organisation of work, equality and diversity in the workplace, health and safety at work, protection of employer's or customer's property and for the purposes of the exercise and enjoyment, on an individual or collective basis, of rights and benefits related to employment, and for the purpose of the termination of the employment relationship.
2. Those rules shall include suitable and specific measures to safeguard the data subject's human dignity, legitimate interests and fundamental rights, with particular regard to the transparency of processing, the transfer of personal data within a group of undertakings, or a group of enterprises engaged in a joint economic activity and monitoring systems at the work place.
3. Each Member State shall notify to the Commission those provisions of its law which it adopts pursuant to paragraph 1, by 25 May 2018 and, without delay, any subsequent amendment affecting them.

Relevant Recital

(155) Processing in the employment context

Article 89 Safeguards and derogations relating to processing for archiving purposes in the public interest, scientific or historical research purposes or statistical purposes

1. Processing for archiving purposes in the public interest, scientific or historical research purposes or statistical purposes, shall be subject to appropriate safeguards, in accordance with this Regulation, for the rights and freedoms of the data subject. Those safeguards shall ensure that technical and organisational measures are in place in particular in order to ensure respect for the principle of data minimisation. Those measures may include pseudonymisation provided that those purposes can be fulfilled in that manner. Where those purposes can be fulfilled by further processing which does not permit or no longer permits the identification of data subjects, those purposes shall be fulfilled in that manner.

2. Where personal data are processed for scientific or historical research purposes or statistical purposes, Union or Member State law may provide for derogations from the rights referred to in Articles 15, 16, 18 and 21 subject to the conditions and safeguards referred to in paragraph 1 of this Article in so far as such rights are likely to render impossible or seriously impair the achievement of the specific purposes, and such derogations are necessary for the fulfilment of those purposes.

3. Where personal data are processed for archiving purposes in the public interest, Union or Member State law may provide for derogations from the rights referred to in Articles 15, 16, 18, 19, 20 and 21 subject to the conditions and safeguards referred to in paragraph 1 of this Article in so far as such rights are likely to render impossible or seriously impair the achievement of the specific purposes, and such derogations are necessary for the fulfilment of those purposes.

4. Where processing referred to in paragraphs 2 and 3 serves at the same time another purpose, the derogations shall apply only to processing for the purposes referred to in those paragraphs.

Relevant Recitals

(156) Processing for archiving, scientific or historical research or statistical purposes

(157) Information from registries and scientific research

(158) Processing for archiving purposes

(159) Processing for scientific research purposes

(160) Processing for historical research purposes

(161) Consenting to the participation in clinical trials

(162) Processing for statistical purposes
(163) Production of European and national statistics

Article 90 Obligations of secrecy

1. Member States may adopt specific rules to set out the powers of the supervisory authorities laid down in points (e) and (f) of Article 58(1) in relation to controllers or processors that are subject, under Union or Member State law or rules established by national competent bodies, to an obligation of professional secrecy or other equivalent obligations of secrecy where this is necessary and proportionate to reconcile the right of the protection of personal data with the obligation of secrecy. Those rules shall apply only with regard to personal data which the controller or processor has received as a result of or has obtained in an activity covered by that obligation of secrecy.
2. Each Member State shall notify to the Commission the rules adopted pursuant to paragraph 1, by 25 May 2018 and, without delay, any subsequent amendment affecting them.

Relevant Recital

(164) Professional or other equivalent secrecy obligations

Article 91 Existing data protection rules of churches and religious associations

1. Where in a Member State, churches and religious associations or communities apply, at the time of entry into force of this Regulation, comprehensive rules relating to the protection of natural persons with regard to processing, such rules may continue to apply, provided that they are brought into line with this Regulation.
2. Churches and religious associations which apply comprehensive rules in accordance with paragraph 1 of this Article shall be subject to the supervision of an independent supervisory authority, which may be specific, provided that it fulfils the conditions laid down in Chapter VI of this Regulation.

Relevant Recital

(165) No prejudice of the status of churches and religious associations

CHAPTER X DELEGATED ACTS AND IMPLEMENTING ACTS

Article 92 Exercise of the Delegation

1. The power to adopt delegated acts is conferred on the Commission subject to the conditions laid down in this Article.
2. The delegation of power referred to in Article 12(8) and Article 43(8) shall be conferred on the Commission for an indeterminate period of time from 24 May 2016.
3. The delegation of power referred to in Article 12(8) and Article 43(8) may be revoked at any time by the European Parliament or by the Council. A decision of revocation shall put an end to the delegation of power specified in that decision. It shall take effect the day following that of its publication in the *Official Journal of the European Union* or at a later date specified therein. It shall not affect the validity of any delegated acts already in force.
4. As soon as it adopts a delegated act, the Commission shall notify it simultaneously to the European Parliament and to the Council.
5. A delegated act adopted pursuant to Article 12(8) and Article 43(8) shall enter into force only if no objection has been expressed by either the European Parliament or the Council within a period of three months of notification of that act to the European Parliament and the Council or if, before the expiry of that period, the European Parliament and the Council have both informed the Commission that they will not object. That period shall be extended by three months at the initiative of the European Parliament or of the Council.

Relevant Recitals

(166) Delegated acts of the Commission
(167) Implementing powers of the Commission
(168) Implementing acts on standard contractual clauses
(169) Immediately applicable implementing acts
(170) Principle of subsidiarity and principle of proportionality

Article 93 Committee Procedure

1. The Commission shall be assisted by a committee. That committee shall be a committee within the meaning of Regulation (EU) No 182/2011.
2. Where reference is made to this paragraph, Article 5 of Regulation (EU) No 182/2011 shall apply.
3. Where reference is made to this paragraph, Article 8 of Regulation ((EU) No 182/2011, in conjunction with Article 5 thereof, shall apply.

CHAPTER XI FINAL PROVISIONS

Article 94 Repeal of Directive 95/46/EC

1.   Directive 95/46/EC is repealed with effect from 25 May 2018.

References to the repealed Directive shall be construed as references to this Regulation. References to the Working Party on the Protection of Individuals with regard to the Processing of Personal Data established by Article 29 of Directive 95/46/EC shall be construed as references to the European Data Protection Board established by this Regulation.

Relevant Recital

(171) Repeal of Directive 95/46/EC and transitional provisions

Article 95 Relationship with Directive 2002/58/EC

This Regulation shall not impose additional obligations on natural or legal persons in relation to processing in connection with the provision of publicly available electronic communications services in public communication networks in the Union in relation to matters for which they are subject to specific obligations with the same objective set out in Directive 2002/58/EC.

Relevant Recital

(173) Relationship to Directive 2002/58/EC

Article 96 Relationship with previously concluded Agreements

International agreements involving the transfer of personal data to third countries or international organisations which were concluded by Member States prior to 24 May 2016, and which comply with Union law as applicable prior to that date, shall remain in force until amended, replaced or revoked.

Article 97 Commission Reports

1.   By 25 May 2020 and every four years thereafter, the Commission shall submit a report on the evaluation and review of this Regulation to the European Parliament and to the Council. The reports shall be made public.

2. In the context of the evaluations and reviews referred to in paragraph 1, the Commission shall examine, in particular, the application and functioning of:

    a) Chapter V on the transfer of personal data to third countries or international organisations with particular regard to decisions adopted pursuant to Article 45(3) of this Regulation and decisions adopted on the basis of Article 25(6) of Directive 95/46/EC;

    b) Chapter VII on cooperation and consistency.

3. For the purpose of paragraph 1, the Commission may request information from Member States and supervisory authorities.

4. In carrying out the evaluations and reviews referred to in paragraphs 1 and 2, the Commission shall take into account the positions and findings of the European Parliament, of the Council, and of other relevant bodies or sources.

5. The Commission shall, if necessary, submit appropriate proposals to amend this Regulation, in particular taking into account of developments in information technology and in the light of the state of progress in the information society.

Article 98 Review of other Union legal acts on data protection

The Commission shall, if appropriate, submit legislative proposals with a view to amending other Union legal acts on the protection of personal data, in order to ensure uniform and consistent protection of natural persons with regard to processing. This shall in particular concern the rules relating to the protection of natural persons with regard to processing by Union institutions, bodies, offices and agencies and on the free movement of such data.

Article 99 Entry into force and application

1. This Regulation shall enter into force on the twentieth day following that of its publication in the Official Journal of the European Union.

2. It shall apply from 25 May 2018.

Index